AUTHOR BIOGRA

Robert Halliday was born in Cambridge, but moved to Bury St. Edmunds with his family in 1966, attending Tollgate Primary School, King Edward VI School and the West Suffolk College in that town. He began exploring historic churches at the age of ten: this interest initially prompted him to investigate gravestones. Holding B.A. and M.A. degrees in history from North London Polytechnic and the State University of New York at Binghampton in the U.S.A., he spends his spare time researching unusual aspects of history and folklore. He is the author of *Cambridge Ghosts* (co-authored with Alan Murdie) and published by arima, *Cambridgeshire Strange But True*, *Suffolk Strange But True* and *Around Bury St. Edmunds in Old Photographs*, as well as articles in popular and academic journals. His other interests include collecting eyebaths (he owns over 150 different specimens). He has recently taken up horseriding.

Suffolk
Graves

GRAVES OF THE FAMOUS AND NOTABLE

Robert Halliday

Published 2019 by arima publishing

www.arimapublishing.com

Revised Second Edition

ISBN 978 1 84549 749 1

© 2019 Robert Halliday

Typeset in Garamond

arima publishing
ASK House, Northgate Avenue
Bury St Edmunds, Suffolk IP32 6BB
t: (+44) 01284 700321
www.arimapublishing.com

This book is dedicated to
the indomitable spirit of Suffolk:
The Suffolk Punch

CONTENTS

INTRODUCTION

This book represents a Suffolk pilgrimage: a journey to discover some of the famous or historically significant people whose gravestones can be found in the churchyards or cemeteries across the county. In 2003, when the idea of writing this book first appeared in my mind, I visited an East Suffolk country church: since the rector happened to be present, I asked him if any special people were buried in the churchyard. 'They are all special people' he replied.

While this statement is true, it would be impractical to write a book that contains every churchyard memorial in Suffolk, so I have limited my selection to monuments of those who have made a significant contribution to the history of Suffolk, or the world in general.

Some of those included here are well known; in a few cases many people visit their graves to honour their memory. Others have achieved distinction within certain fields of endeavour. Others are even little known within the community where their remains are laid to rest, but may be worthy of deserve greater appreciation. My hope is that those reading this book may recognise the incredible historical inheritance to be found in some unexpected places in Suffolk.

ACKNOWLEDGEMENTS

In the preparation of this book, thanks are due to Martin Mellett, who helped put the idea into my mind in the first place; Dr John Ridgard, who ran a local history class which introduced me to some of the people mentioned in this book (in particular Goodwyn Barmby); and Paul Scott, the Grounds Maintenance Supervisor at Ipswich Cemetery for a very inspiring and informative tour of the historic and unusual graves there. Jeremy Apter of Little Cornard provided information on Cyril ('Monty') Bowers; Rob Butterworth of Bury St. Edmunds supplied a detailed biography of John Orridge; Sam Hare of Sudbury told me about Ron Greenwood's grave in Sudbury cemetery; Stephen Mael of the Long Shop Museum at Leiston sent crucial details about the Garrett family memorial at Carlton; Andrew Palmer of the William Alwyn Society sent a quote from that composer's diary; the Rev. Tony Redman of Great Livermere told me about Vladimir Peniakov ('Popski')'s gravestone at Wixoe; and Els Tompkins of Sue Ryder provided essential information on the residents of the Sue Ryder Home buried in Cavendish cemetery. In my explorations and adventures in the preparation of this book I was greatly assisted by Jeremy Hobson, Alan Murdie and Andrew Snowdon, while my aunt Eileen of Port Washington, Long Island, U.S.A, was a constant source of encouragement throughout.

Edward Fitzgerald's interpretation of *The Rubiyat Of Omar Khayyam* has made his grave in Boulge churchyard an object of pilgrimage. Born in Bredfield Hall to wealthy family, he lived as a 'genteel gypsy', moving between rented lodgings, when his family acquired Boulge Hall he preferred to live in a cottage in the grounds. If his unconventional appearance and behaviour made him an object of amusement, or even hostility, he developed intense friendshps, forming an informal social circle of local literary and artistic enthusiasts, the 'Woodbridge wits': his letters to people he knew are regarded as brilliant literary expressions. Owning a yacht he called *Scandal* (saying this travelled faster than anything else in Woodbridge), he socialised with Suffolk fishermen and studied maritime dialect.

Reticent about his abilities, Edward Fitzgerald only published a small selection of verse. For a pastime he translated foreign literature, seeing to capture a work's 'essence' rather than write a full and literal version. He studied *The Rubiyat Of Omar Khayyam*, a medieval Persian anthology of 1,000 aphorisms, which he collated into a 75 stanza poem. Only 250 copies were printed, when none were sold the publisher put them in a 'penny box'. Whitley Stokes, a literary scholar, passed by and bought a copy. Captivated by its poetic brilliance, Whitley Stokes read it to friends, including the 'Pre-Raphaelite brotherhood', who were so impressed that they bought copies. Eventually perhaps every British family who enjoyed poetry acquired a copy of the *Rubiayat*, which remains the most widely read and quoted poetic work of the Victorian era. Although Edward did nothing to capitalise on the *Rubiayat's* success, he was projected from an obscure local eccentric into a pivotal figure of Suffolk local history, English literature, and the European understanding of Islam.

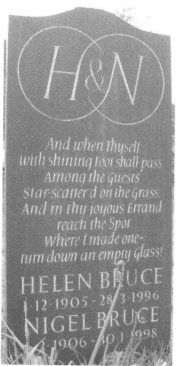

Edward disagreed with his family, especially his brother John, on religion and other matters. He therefore asked to be buried outside the family mausoleum in Boulge churchyard, saying he wished to be closer to nature. His epitaph, 'it is he that has made us and not we ourselves' (Psalm 100: 3) was a riposte to a Woodbridge butcher who claimed to be a self-made man and superior to Edward, whose family were wealthy. William Simpson, the artist, journalist and traveller, took hips from a rose on Omar Khayyam's grave in Nishapur. Admirers of the *Rubaiyat* formed the *Omar Khayyam Club* (still active): in 1893 they planted a rose grown from these hips by Edward's grave, England's oldest rose bush. In 1972 the Iranian ambassador planted new roses nearby. Boulge churchyard contains many tasteful and well-crafted memorials, and should be an essential destination for churchyard enthusiasts. (See *A History of Suffolk Gravestones*, page 83.)

A gravestone at Hollesley displays the final verse of Edward Fitzgerald's translation of *The Rubaiyat*.

James Chambers was born in Soham in 1748. A tradesman's son, he chose to become a tramp, dressed in rags and followed by dogs, often living in homemade shacks. Teaching himself to read and write, he made money composing impromptu verses for people, such as 'acrostics' from the letters of their names: one about himself began:

> James Chambers is my name,
> And I am scorned by rich and poor,
> Many a weary step I came,
> Enduring hardships very sore,
> So I design to take a wife,
> Can I but have one to my mind
> Henceforth to live a better life
> And then we may true solace find

A collection of his poetry, with his biography and portrait, was published in 1820. He died one winter sheltering in an empty farmhouse at Stradbroke, villagers paid for a gravestone in Stradbroke churchyard.

James Bird, the son of a farmer at Earl Stonham, became a miller at Yoxford. Falling into debt he sold the mill and opened a shop. He published book-length poems, including *The Vale of Slaughden*, about the Viking raids; *Dunwich: a Tale of the Splendid City*, and *Framlingham, a Narrative of the Castle*. Melodramatic and fanciful, rather than accurate history, these were the first verse narratives about medieval Suffolk. Another of his works, *The Emigrant's Tale*, may contain autobiographical episodes. He wrote plays, which enjoyed brief 'runs' in London. Local folklore held that James was impecunious, but sustained himself by an infectious sense of humour, often about his own difficulties,

and an ability to make friends. Hearing of James Bird's passing Goodwyn Barmby, a fellow native of Yoxford (see pages 95-6) composed a poem that appeared in the *Ipswich Journal* of 13 April 1839, which includes such lines as:

> Ye sweet valleys of Suffolk! Oh wither your green?
> Let your hills be as dark as when twilight is gloaming...
> ...For he who sang sweetly, the **Bird** of your land,
> Like a halcyon has left you for sunnier strand.

Eleven of James Bird's sixteen children reached maturity. Some (perhaps reacting against his pecuniary difficulties) achieved financial success, and paid for this memorial to be placed over his grave in Yoxford churchyard.

Bernard Barton was born to a Quaker family in Carlisle. As an orphan, relations sent him to boarding school in Ipswich; he became a clerk at Alexander's Bank in Woodbridge (a Quaker business), living in a cottage in Cumberland Street which is one of that town's more attractive small buildings. Writing poems about anything that moved or interested him, he published numerous volumes of verse, pamphlets and contributions to magazines. He sent copies to all whom he thought might enjoy them, including the poets Charles Lamb and Robert Southey, with whom he maintained correspondence. This self-promotion had some results: after receiving his poems Robert Peel secured him an annual pension. Bernard belonged to Edward Fitzgerald's 'Woodbridge Wits'; (see pages 5-6) on his death Edward re-edited his poetry, which even his closest friends agreed placed quantity over quality. His gravestone in the Quaker cemetery at Turn Lane in Woodbridge demonstrates the Quaker convention of reckoning days and months by numbers, as Quakers thought the traditional names honoured pagan deities. (See *A History of Suffolk Gravestones* page 71.)

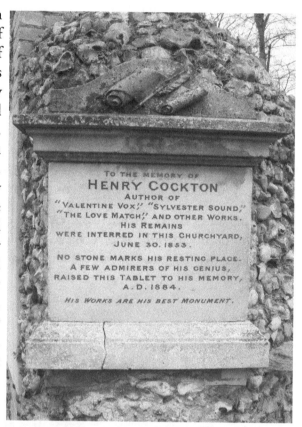

Henry Cockton was born in London, but married Ann Howes of Bury St. Edmunds and spent much of his life there. His fame rests on his first novel, *Valentine Vox*, the story of a ventriloquist who learns the skill in a Suffolk town (clearly Bury St. Edmunds) before moving to London to enjoy many amusing escapades. (The comedy is complemented by a sub-plot about Valentine's uncle Grimwood, who is unjustly confined in a lunatic asylum, the first literary study of a sane person unjustly classed as insane.) *Valentine Vox* sold over 400,000 copies, and briefly rivalled Charles Dickens for popularity (although the humour has dated badly). Henry Cockton wrote eight further novels, some set in Suffolk, but failed to secure the copyright and made little profit from them. He lost his money (and health) after some disastrous financial ventures: at the end of his life he became synonymous with misfortune. He was buried in an unmarked grave; in 1884 some admirers subscribed to place this memorial on the charnel house in the Great Churchyard in Bury St. Edmunds.

Mary Theresa Vidal went to Australia in 1840, aged 25, when her husband took a post as a clergyman in New South Wales. Here she wrote two books with Australian settings: *Tales From The Bush* and *The Cabramatta Store*. *The Convict Laundress*, a story from the first volume, was published separately and enjoyed further success. Returning to England she wrote *Bengala*, another fictional work about New South Wales. While her works are largely forgotten, she can be claimed as Australia's first female novelist. Her husband became vicar of Sutton, where she was buried in the churchyard.

Agnes and Jane Strickland were brought up at Reydon Hall, part of a family of eight brothers and sisters, six of whom became authors. Between 1840 and 1848 Agnes and her sister Elizabeth published a ten volume *History of the Queens of England* which they researched from contemporary source material (having to petition the government for access to the State Paper Office, which then refused to admit women). Based on a self-proclaimed maxim 'facts not opinions', this was among the most popular historical works

of the time. The reticent Elizabeth did not wish for an author's credit, leaving the more socially confident Agnes to be lionised by the literary and social world. Agnes produced other works about the queens of Scotland (in particular her personal heroine, Mary Queen of Scots) and the Tudor and Stuart princesses. The Stricklands prepared the way for later generations of women's historians, blazing a trail through a widespread prejudice against women in academia. Elizabeth moved to Kent, but Agnes was buried in Southwold churchyard, northeast of the church, under the lower monument (foreground) naming her as the 'historian of the Queens of England'. Jane, Agnes's younger sister, wrote *Rome, Regal and Republican*, a popular textbook history, and sixteen novels with moral themes, including *Adonijah*, about a Jew who lived in the time of Jesus, as well as Agnes's biography. Jane was buried under the taller memorial (background).

Richard Cobbold was rector of Wortham: although his father, a wealthy Ipswich brewer, bought the post for him, he was a model clergyman, dedicated to his parish and parishioners. He wrote novels including *The History of Margaret Catchpole*, which remains in print to this day. Margaret Catchpole had been the Cobbold family's servant (she may have saved Richard from drowning as an infant) but fell foul of the law and was transported to Australia, where she reformed to become a model citizen. Richard was brought up with stories of Margaret's adventures, which he romanticised for a semi-fictional biography, dramatised several times, most recently by the Ipswich based Eastern Angles Theatre Company. If *The History of Margaret Catchpole* suffers from extensive moralising, it could be described as 'the great Suffolk novel' (it includes digressions on the Suffolk landscape and local history). Other works include *Mary Ann Wellington*, about a soldier's widow, highlighting the injustices of the poor law system, and *Freston Tower*, a historical romance, which although fictional, is often thought to be fact. He helped fellow clergyman John Heigham Steggall write *The Suffolk Gypsy*. An amateur artist, Richard Cobbold painted pictures and wrote character sketches of his parishioners, a unique record of a Victorian rural community, published in 2007 as *Parson and People in a Suffolk Village* edited by David Dymond. He is buried near the war memorial in Wortham churchyard.

Orlando Whistlecraft was a native of Thwaite. Childhood illnesses left him in poor physical health, but he received sufficient education to run a village school. After publishing *The Climate of England* in 1840 he devoted himself to meteorology. His annual *Whistlecraft's Weather Almanacs*, which included his poems and observations on other subjects, were extremely popular. He was buried in Thwaite churchyard. The M. R. James ghost story *Rats* refers to his weather records.

Florence Henniker was born Florence Milnes, the daughter of a aristocratic parents, Florence Nightingale, a family friend, was her godmother. She married Arthur Henry Henniker Major of Thornham Park. She wrote six novels, two collections of short stories, and a play, *The Courage Of Silence*, but is better known for her relationship with Thomas Hardy. They met in Dublin in 1893, when he fell in love with her. She rejected Hardy's amorous advances, but they remained friends, collaborating in writing a short

story *The Spectre Of The Real*; letters they exchanged have been published and enjoyed by Hardy enthusiasts. Florence was the 'one rare fair woman' in Hardy's poem *Wessex Heights* and the inspiration for Sue Bridehead in *Jude The Obscure*. Her grave in Thornham Magna churchyard is somewhat in need of attention. (See *A History of Suffolk Gravestones* pages 95-6.)

Julian Tennyson, the great-grandson of Alfred, Lord Tennyson, was born in London in 1915, and began visiting Suffolk when his family holidayed there. At 23 he wrote *Suffolk Scene*, a brilliantly observed book about the essential spirit of places and things in the county. Enlisting in the army with the onset of the Second World War, he was killed by flying shrapnel in the Battle of Arakan in Burma in 1945. He wrote about the beauty of Iken, his favourite place:

When I was a child I decided that here was the place for me to be buried. I have not altered my mind. Everyone wants to lie in his own country: this is mine. I shall feel safe if I have the scream of birds and the moan of the wind and the lapping of the water all round me, and the lonely woods and marshes that I know so well. How can anyone say what he will feel when he is dead? What I mean is that I shall feel secure in dying.

While his resting place is the Taukkyan War Cemetery in Myanmar (Burma), his daughter had this headstone erected at Iken in 2007.

People admiring Julian Tennyson's grave on a pilgrimage to Iken, in which the author participated, in October 2010.

John Middleton Murry's father was fiercely ambitious that he should achieve success by education, and gave him intensive home tuition that earned him a scholarship to Oxford University. John then left Oxford to pursue a personal and professional relationship with the authoress Katherine Mansfield, which developed into an intense and turbulent ménage with D. H. and Frieda Lawrence (John and Katherine inspired

Gudrun and Gerald in D. H. Lawrence's *Women in Love*). Katherine Mansfield died in 1923: although John re-married three times she overshadowed the rest of his life. One of the twentieth century's most prolific literary critics, he wrote perhaps a hundred books and innumerable articles. He founded and edited the influential journal *Adelphi*, which gave George Orwell early publicity. Involvement in socialism and pacifism led him to start an experimental agricultural community at Thelnetham. He was buried on the east side of Thelnetham churchyard; his fourth wife was later buried beside him. The quote 'ripeness is all' (*King Lear*, act 5 scene 2) summarised his attitude to life in his final years. (R. (Reginald) Allen Brown, a historian who produced seminal works on the Norman Conquest, is buried on the west side of Thelnetham churchyard.)

Edmund Blunden's plans to study at Oxford were cut short by the First World War. Enlisting in the army he served on the Western Front, where the destruction of men (and countryside) that he witnessed left indelible scars on his mind, as shown by much of his work, including his autobiographical *Undertones of War*, regarded as one of the best prose narratives of the conflict. He was awarded the Military Cross, although, unusually for a junior officer he received no physical wounds (he said his short stature made him a difficult target). Holding university posts in Hong Kong, Japan and Oxford, he wrote over 1,000 poems, as well as studies of other writers (and a book about his love of cricket). Discovering unpublished poems by John Clare and Wilfred Owen, he was awarded the C.B.E. for services to literature. His love of Suffolk began when

stationed at Stowlangtoft after demobilisation. Late in life he settled at Hall Mill in Long Melford; he was buried at the east end of Long Melford churchyard. The lines on the stone, 'I live still to love still things quiet and unconcerned' come from his poem *Seers*. Edmund Blunden is one of First World War poets honoured on a memorial in Poet's Corner in Westminster Abbey, among whom he saw the longest period of active service and lived the longest after the war.

Adrian Bell was a journalist's son who decided to work in agriculture. A highly capable Suffolk farmer, he wrote books known for meticulous observations of rural life, describing mechanisation of agriculture without rancour or sentiment. He produced the first *Times* crossword (and over 4,000 more). Retiring to Beccles, he was buried at Barsham.

Norah Lofts was born Norah Robinson at Shipdam in Norfolk. When she was nine her family moved to Bury St. Edmunds, which she regarded as her ideal town. After attending the Guildhall Feoffment and County Grammar Schools, she qualified as a teacher in Norwich (her only prolonged absence from Bury St. Edmunds). Returning to become a teacher at the Guildhall Feoffment School, she married Geoffrey Lofts. Her first book, *I Met A Gypsy* received five years of rejections, before being accepted for publication. Good sales in Britain and the U.S.A. prompted her to become a full-time writer. She produced over fifty books, mainly romances or biographical novels with historical themes. These included

'roman a clef' works set in Bury St. Edmunds (re-named Baildon), most notably her *Suffolk Trilogy: The Town House, The House At Old Vine* and *The House At Sunset*. She did not avoid difficult subjects: a later novel, *The Claw*, described a community terrorised by a psychopath. She wrote murder mysteries under the name Peter Curtis; nonfiction historical studies; and re-interpretations of Bible stories. Some of her books were adapted as films, most notably *Jassy*, starring Margaret Lockwood and Dennis Price, as well as *Guilt Is My Shadow*; the 'Hammer Horror' *The Witches*, and *Seven Women* (the last film directed by John Ford). After Geoffrey Lofts died she re-married Dr. Robert Jorisch, a chemist who helped to set up the town's Sugar Beet factory, they moved to Northgate House in Northgate Street, her home for the rest of her life, where there is a commemorative plaque to her. She was an independent town councillor for Bury St. Edmunds between 1957 and 1962, when she acted to save the Corn Exchange and other historic buildings from demolition. Her grave can be found in Bury St. Edmunds Cemetery, south of the West Road entrance, opposite the junction of West Road and Linnet Road.

Elizabeth Smart was born in Ottawa. She showed early promise as a pianist, but rebelled against her background to live a 'Bohemian' existence with unconventional writers and intellectuals. Convinced that only love would make her realise her literary potential, after she read poetry by George Granville Barker, then living in Japan, she sent him the money for a plane trip to meet her: they embarked on a volatile affair (oblivious to the fact that George was already married). This relationship inspired her angst-ridden prose poem *By Grand Central Station I Sat Down and Wept*, which has a cult following. Admirers include the singer Morrissey, who has used quotes from it in his songs. In the 1960's she bought a cottage at Flixton called *The Dell* where she channelled her energies into cultivating a garden, which, she felt, revived her creative drive. Her memoirs, *In The Meantime* furthered her reputation. She was buried in the churchyard of St. George's church at South Elmham St. Cross: the epitaph 'non omnis moriar', a quote from Horace, means 'I will not die altogether'. South Elmham St. Cross churchyard overlooks a small river valley, and is an exceptionally tranquil stopping point to visit and relax in.

Arthur Leslie (A. L.) Morton was a Marxist historian. The son of a farmer at Hengrave, he studied at Cambridge. He was effectively dismissed as a public school teacher after supporting railway workers during the National Strike. He then taught at Summerhill, A. S. Neill's 'progressive school' at Leiston (see page 94). A member of the Communist party, a journalist for the *Daily Worker*, and a participant in the 'Hunger Marches' of the 1930's, he was an urban district councillor for Leiston (one of the few English towns with a Communist controlled local authority). His most famous work, *A People's History of England*, emphasised the ordinary people's role in shaping the past. In 1950 he bought a medieval leper chapel at Clare which had been converted into a house, where he wrote poetry and studies of English visionary thinkers and movements. He was buried in the public cemetery, opposite the parish church, in Clare High Street. The epitaph

> Man grows with time
> in grace and gentleness,
> Takes nature's mould
> And nature his.

Comes from his poem *Cokaigne Fantasy*.

Robert John Unstead took up writing after winning a prize for an essay on the British Empire as a nine year old cub scout. As a schoolteacher, he objected to most historical text books. This prompted him to write *Looking at History*, concentrating on everyday events and things, which sold more than eight million copies. He produced over fifty further books on history, mostly, but not exclusively, aimed at children: many were best sellers (read for pleasure as well as school work). Retiring to Aldringham, he is buried in the churchyard there.

John Harold Plumb was the son of a Leicester factory worker. He took a first class honours degree at Leicester University, from which he moved to Cambridge to take a Ph.D. He had a distinguished career at Cambridge (interrupted by service as a code-breaker at Bletchley during the Second World War) becoming Master of Christ's College and Professor of Modern English History. His students included Simon Schama. Specialising in the eighteenth century, he wrote acclaimed studies of history (some were international best sellers). Knighted in 1982, his eightieth birthday saw him honoured with a champagne party at Kensington palace and a reception in the U.S. Congress. He was buried at Westhorpe, where he owned a country house.

Christine Pullein-Thompson, and her sisters Josephine and Diana opened a riding school while they were teenagers; they became the most prolific and best-known exponents of the 'pony story' genre of children's fiction. Christine wrote over 100 books about riding and horse care, (and more in collaboration with her sisters). She lived in Mellis, where she became chairman of the parish council. An active supporter of 'riding for the disabled' she instituted a bridleways group in the area. When I first saw her headstone in Mellis churchyard I found a plastic toy horse on the plinth.

Michael Hamburger was born in Germany to a secular Jewish family who had the foresight to emigrate to Britain in 1933. An original and acclaimed poet, and a gifted translator of German, he held university posts in England and the USA. He retired to Middleton, where he cultivated rare varieties of apple trees; many of his later poems celebrate the Suffolk landscape. He is buried in Middleton churchyard.

17

Two novelists are buried in a modern extension of Kersey churchyard. Ralph Hammond Innes, better known as Hammond Innes, made his reputation (and fortune) with *The Wreck of the Mary Deare*, an international bestseller, followed by a series of adventure stories about protagonists combatting the forces of nature in exotic locations. Many sold over two million copies, some were filmed. He wrote popular books about travel and exploration, including a guide to East Anglia. Living at Ayres End in Kersey, he was active in a campaign to restore Kersey church. Developing a concern for the environment (his later books involve ecological topics) he financed the restoration of derelict woodland at Kersey, and the planting of a million trees in different parts of the world. He was awarded the C.B.E. for his achievements as an author and his public service. An accomplished yachtsman, he left over half his fortune to the Association of Sea Training Organisations, which regards him as one of their most generous benefactors.

Peter Vansittart left Oxford University during the Second World War, being dissatisfied with the degree course. Declared medically unfit for military service he worked for civil defence. He then taught in progressive schools before becoming a full-time writer, producing novels about the development of myths and legends, and studies of history, including his best known and most successful work, *Voices from the Great War*. His reminiscences of an unconventional lifestyle and his wide circle of literary acquaintances made him an accomplished raconteur, inspiring stimulating autobiographies and semi-biographical novels. He received the O.B.E. for services to literature. He inherited a house in Kersey from his mother. Just after I discovered his grave I met a local resident in the churchyard who said he was known locally for walking everywhere: eschewing cars (or a bicycle) and refusing offers of lifts from passers-by.

Henry Walton, the son of a famer from Dickleburgh, became a painter of portraits and miniatures. Working for much of his career in Suffolk, the engraving of his portrait of the first Marquess Cornwallis, the Suffolk landowner and general, was said to hang in virtually every household in the county. Other clients included Horace Walpole and Edward Gibbon. He advised Richard, Viscount Fitzwilliam (the founder of the Fitzwilliam Museum in Cambridge) on forming an art collection. He was buried on the south of Brome church.

Thomas Churchyard was a solicitor in Woodbridge. An expert in the game laws, he was known as 'the poacher's lawyer'. A member of Edward Fitzgerald's 'Woodbridge wits', (see pages 5-6) he was a self-taught artist, who unsuccessfully aspired to become a professional painter. Running into financial difficulties in his sixties, he was bankrupt by the time of his death, when he was buried in his family's home village of Melton. His reputation has grown, and his East Anglian landscapes are now highly praised. Some of his works hang in Christchurch Mansion in Ipswich and Woodbridge Museum.

John Seymour Lucas was a highly successful Victorian historical painter; he designed sets for the theatrical impresario Henry Irving. When travelling in Spain he suffered from a railway accident: thinking he received inadequate compensation he took private revenge by painting the defeat of the Spanish Armada. He lived in *The Priory* at Blythburgh, a medieval building on the site of a monastery, embellishing it with such

success that architectural historians are unsure which parts are genuinely medieval and which parts he added. He was buried in Blythburgh churchyard with his French born wife, Marie Elizabeth Cornelissen, herself an accomplished artist.

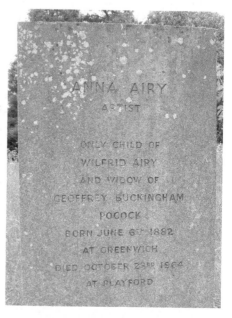

Anna Airy was a native of Playford, the granddaughter of the astronomer George Biddell Airy (see page 85). A star pupil at the Slade School, she was a war artist during the First World War, her paintings of factory workers are among the finest works of the genre. She is buried in Playford churchyard; her artist husband, Geoffrey Buckingham Pocock, and her father, Wilfrid Airy (an engineer, who designed the observatory at Nacton Park) are buried beside her.

Cedric Morris belonged to a wealthy Welsh family (who developed the Morriston district of Swansea): he acquired the title 'Sir Cedric Morris' when he succeeded his father as a baronet. After an honourable discharge from military service during the First World War he became an artist, producing highly observed paintings of flowers and gardens. Proud of his Welsh origins, during the Depression he taught art at an educational settlement near Merthyr Tydfil. With his lifelong partner, Arthur Lett-Haines, he founded the East Anglian School of Painting and Drawing which they moved to Benton End in Hadleigh in 1940: pupils included Lucien Freud and Maggi Hambling. Cedric was a respected botanist, specialising in breeding irises, an iris appears on his gravestone in the cemetery in Friars Road in Hadleigh.

Cornelius 'Cor' Visser was born in Spaarndam in the Netherlands. His paintings were exhibited widely while he was a teenager. Spending much of his early adult life living on houseboats, in 1937 he and his wife Emmy sailed across the North Sea to the Orwell Estuary They saw Pin Mill, the boating harbour at Chelmondiston, whose beauty so impressed them that they made it their home. During the Second World War he became the official war artist for the Dutch government in exile. After Emmy's death he lived in Fore Street in Ipswich, where he founded the Ipswich Rangers Art Club (now the Orwell Art Club): there is a commemorative blue plaque on the building. He and Emmy are buried in Wherstead churchyard, from where there is a splendid view of the Orwell estuary that inspired much of his career.

Margaret Mellis and Francis Davison were abstract artists. Margaret won an art scholarship to Paris as a teenager. She married the poet and artist Adrian Stokes: with Barbara Hepworth and Ben Nicholson they were pioneers of the artistic migration to St. Ives in Cornwall. Frictions and tensions within the St. Ives community caused Adrian to abandon Margaret, who contemplated suicide. She was rescued from despair by Francis Davison, who moved to Cornwall after a divorce. Marrying in 1948, they created collages from found objects: moving to Suffolk, they used a fisherman's shack at Walberswick as a studio and source of inspiration. Two years after Francis's death Margaret received a letter from an aspiring young artist called Damien Hirst, who she provided with early tuition. Margaret was a local 'character' swimming in the sea and cycling local roads into her eighties. Francis and Margaret were buried at Walberswick.

'Carl' Giles was born Ronald Giles: teenage jibes that he resembled the horror film actor Boris Karloff resulted in the nickname 'Karlo', shortened to 'Carl'. At 26 he became a cartoonist for the *Sunday* and *Daily Express*. He was a war artist during the Second World war (exempted from military service because of partial deafness and poor eyesight). At the end of the war he created 'the Giles family' a cartoon feature for the *Sunday* and *Daily Express*, about an extended lower-middle class group of relatives (overshadowed by the truculent 'Grandma Giles') coping with wartime austerity measures. Never aging, the Giles family adapted to changing times as the decades rolled on, making wry comments on social and political issues. Every year Carl's cartoons were republished in the *Giles Annuals* which remain highly collectable. Carl married his cousin, and childhood sweetheart, Joan: they lived in Witnesham. A keen boating enthusiast on the Orwell, he designed fund-raising Christmas Cards for the Royal National Lifeboat Association (R.N.L.I.) who so appreciated his support that he was elected president of the organisation. Receiving the O.B.E. for services to art and charity fundraising, after his retirement from newspaper work a statue of 'Grandma Giles' with other characters from the Giles family was unveiled outside his former studio in Princes Street in Ipswich. Dying from complications caused by diabetes, he was buried at Tuddenham St. Martin, near Ipswich, where his gravestone gives his nickname rather than his actual name. Anthologies of his cartoons remain popular.

The Rope family, who originated in Blaxhall, produced distinguished writers and artists. Ellen Mary Rope, an acclaimed exponent of bas relief sculpture, was a designer for the Della Robbia pottery and member of the Arts and Crafts Exhibition Society. Admirers in fin-de-siècle Paris called her 'the poet sculptor'. Retiring to Blaxhall, she was buried alongside members of her family near the church porch. Examples of her sculpture can be seen in the church.

Margaret Edith Rope, a stained glass artist, was born in Leiston, the daughter of Ellen Mary's brother Arthur. Amazingly her cousin, Margaret

Agnes Rope, pursued a similar career. They studied together in The Glass House at Fulham, where Margaret Edith was known as 'Tor' (from a childhood nickname of 'tortoise', an animal she sometimes included in her windows as a 'signature'), while Margaret Agnes was known as 'Marga'. Both were born

Anglicans; Marga converted to Roman Catholicism to become a nun in the convent at Quidenham; Tor converted after designing windows there. Tor made windows for churches in 23 English counties, as well as Australia and Trinidad. In Suffolk her work can be seen at Barnby, Earl Soham, and impressively at Leiston, in a tour-de-force incorporating Suffolk Punches at work. Sadly Tor's last years were devastated by Alzheimer's disease; she was buried at the Holy Family and St. Michael Roman Catholic Church at Kesgrave. This church, which contains stained glass by Tor and Marga, and sculpture by Ellen Mary, was built in memory of Marga's brother Michael. Also a convert to Roman Catholicism, Michael was an aircraft engineer who was killed in the R101 disaster (when Britain's largest ever airship crashed). Michael's widow, Lucy Rope (nee Jolly), the foundress of the church, buried beside Tor, devoted her life to fund raising for charitable causes, including the promotion of the public understanding of science.

Cecil Howard Lay was the son of the village schoolmaster at Aldringham. After military service during the First World War he spent his life in Aldringham. He produced art nouveau prints and paintings, before changing to paint local scenes in a pseudo-naïve style. In his forties and fifties he wrote poetry in the 'Georgian' vogue, which remains surprisingly little known, despite its lyric and stylistic quality. He designed houses in the Aldringham area. Outside of his artistic accomplishments, he studied his pet tortoise, making important zoological research by observing its annual routine. He is buried under a rather worn headstone in his home village.

Henry Munro Cautley worked as an architect in Cornhill Chambers in Ipswich in partnership with Leslie Barefoot (see page 30). His commissions included Ipswich Public Library in Northgate Street, a successful blend of art nouveau and mock-Tudor. Surveyor to the diocese of St. Edmundsbury and Ipswich, he supervised church restorations in Suffolk, and was resposible for three churches in Ipswich (All Hallows, St. Andrew and St. Augustine of Hippo). He is best known as the author of *Suffolk Churches And Their Treasures*, one of the most important books about Suffolk church art and architecture. Living at Westerfield (where his father had been rector) he was buried in the churchyard there, under a gravestone which he designed himself.

Basil Spence showed such outstanding early ability as an architect that his services were already in demand while he was a student. He attained international fame after designing the new cathedral at Coventry, which won him a knighthood, the Order of Merit, and the presidency of the Royal Institute of British Architects. This was the last example of modern architecture in Britain that people actually travelled to see. (I remember going with my parents to see Coventry Cathedral when I was seven, which was even before my own interest in churches started; one memory of my primary school days is a Canadian teacher on exchange telling my class how he had taken his family to see it.) His later works include the University of Sussex, the British Embassy in Rome and an extension of the New Zealand Parliament building in Wellington, (called

The Beehive). Basil Spence retired to Yaxley Hall and was buried at Thornham Parva under a large memorial which reproduces an architectural drawing board. His later works have been castigated as prime examples of what is facetiously called 'brutalism'. Nevertheless, Coventry Cathedral remains a paradigm of modern architecture.

One of the most surprising discoveries I made when researching this book was the grave of the film producer, director and scriptwriter Emeric Pressburger in the rather remote and little visited churchyard at Aspall. Born to a Hungarian Jewish family, Emeric Pressburer enjoyed success in the Berlin cinema industry, until the rise of Hitler caused him to move to France, and finally to England. Here he formed a remarkable partnership with Michael Powell. Emeric Pressburger and Michael Powell created nineteen films notable for elaborate sets, fantasy sequences and cinematic spectacle. In many ways these were ahead of the times, not just of the expectations of the cinema-going public, but even the critical establishment. Three of their films were awarded 'Oscars': *49th Parallel*, an attack on Nazism, symbolised by a small group of Nazi soldiers; *Black Narcissus*, about nuns on a mission in Tibet, with some of the most spectacular studio sets of the pre-computer age (courting disapproval by showing a religious community fatally disrupted by psychological tension) and *The Red Shoes*, perhaps the most spectacular film about ballet ever made. Their other collaborations included *A Matter of Life and Death* which portrayed a trial held in heaven, to decide whether a wounded airman should be allowed to live or die. Powell and Pressburger's portrayal of the British military establishment in *The Life and Death of Colonel Blimp* continues to provoke controversy. In 1969 Emeric Pressburger bought 'Shoemaker's Cottage' in Aspall as a retirement home. He asked to be buried at Aspall, his grave lies northwest of the church. Martin Scorsese, a great admirer, sent flowers to his funeral. A 'star of David' was carved on the memorial (the only such use of this emblem in a Church of England churchyard). The epitaph

> Love rules the court, the camp, the grove,
> This world below and heaven above,
> For love is heaven, and heaven is love

comes from Walter Scott's poem *The Lay of the Last Minstrel*, featured in *A Matter of Life and Death*.

Frederick Ashton was born in South America to English ex-patriate parents. He was inspired to become a ballet dancer after seeing Anna Pavlova. Returning to England he became a dancer and choreographer. With Marie Rambert he formed the dance company which became The Royal Ballet. He promoted Margot Fonteyn's career, and revolutionised standards with ballets he devised himself, and re-interpretations of existing productions. He choreographed the film *Tales Of Beatrix Potter*, one of the most popular cinematic adaptations of ballet, in which he played the eponymous hedgehog from *The Tale Of Miss Tiggywinkle*. His achievements were recognised with a knighthood, and admission into the British Order of Merit, the French Legion d'Honneur and Danish Order of Dannebrog. His mother's family came from Yaxley, this prompted him to acquire Chandos Lodge at Eye and Church Cottage at Yaxley. He was buried at Yaxley; the hedgehog on his gravestone commemorates his performance as Miss Tiggywinkle.

Angus McBean was Britain's leading theatrical photographer. His images of Audrey Hepburn boosted her early career; his portrait of Vivien Leigh, which he regarded as his finest work, appeared on a British postage stamp in 1985. His best known photograph must be the cover of *Please Please Me*, the Beatles' massively successful debut album. He retired to Flemings Hall at Bedingfield, and was buried in the modern public cemetery in Debenham, between Aspall Road and Priory Lane. Angus McBean's technical and artistic ability was such that he could be considered the most important British photographer of the twentieth century. The epitaph is an extract from Henry Wadsworth Longfellow's *Psalm of Life*.

Peter Fuller was an influential, but contraversial art critic. His early work supported modern artistic movements. In the 1980's his changed his attitudes, espousing the ideals of the Victorian thinker John Ruskin. He founded the journal *Modern Painters* (named after one of Ruskin's books) to expound his new theories, making vitriolic attacks on some of the more extreme developments of modern art. Contributors to *Modern Painters* included Sister Wendy Beckett, whose early career as an art critic he encouraged, and the pop singer David Bowie. At 42 he died in a tragic car accident when his pregnant wife was injured, and their unborn child, posthumously called Gabriel, was killed. Peter Fuller was buried in Stowlangtoft, where he had a country cottage. He promoted landscape art for its mystic significance; the sculptor Glynn Williams, whom he championed, produced this memorial, which assumes a different form from whichever angle it is seen. Buds rising into flower symbolise Peter and Gabriel's premature deaths, and represent spring, the renewal of nature, rebirth and resurrection.

Simon Cadell was an actor, whose most famous role was in the television comedy *Hi-De-Hi*, where he played Jeffrey Fairbrother, a university professor who became an entertainment officer at a holiday camp (the series was co-written by David Croft, who lived at Honington). Simon married David Croft's daughter, Rebecca, and starred in *Life Without George*, a 'sitcom' written by Rebecca's sister, Penny. On his early death at 46 he was buried in Honington churchyard, under a headstone bearing a poignant quote 'our revels now are ended' from Shakespeare's *The Tempest*.

Jean Kent was born Joan Mildred Summerfield to actor parents. Taking the stage name Jean Kent, she followed her parents' stage career. Spotted by Gainsborough Pictures talent scouts, she established a reputation as a *femme fatale* in *Fanny By Gaslight*, *Waterloo Road* and *The Wicked Lady*. In 1946, aged twenty five, she received top billing in *Caravan*, above Stewart Granger. She was a box office draw in *Tottie True* (also titled *The Gay Lady*, her personal favourite), *Sleeping Car To Trieste*, *The Reluctant Widow* and *The Woman In Question*. Through the 1950's she continued to be sought after in supporting roles (playing Janet Halliday

in *Please Turn Over*, a personal favourite of mine, since it is about a Halliday family)! After 1960 she remained active on television, playing Queen Elizabeth in the adventure series *Sir Francis Drake*, and appearing in *Two's Company*, a 1970 episode of the comedy classic *Steptoe And Son* as the love interest of both Harold/Harry H. Corbett and Albert/ Wilfred Brambell.

Jusuf Ramart was born in Austria to a family of Albanian origin. Coming to England after the Second World War, he worked on the fringe of the cinema industry, meeting Jean Kent as Stewart Granger's stunt double in *Caravan*. (He was an expert horse rider.) Stewart Granger was best man at Jean and Jusuf's wedding. Taking the English surname Hurst, he abandoned cinema to become a property developer.

Jean Kent only made occasional film or television appearances from her sixties. Moving to a country home in Westhorpe, she was buried in the churchyard there.

William Middleditch was born in Hawkedon. He served with the First Foot Guards in the Walcheren expedition, the Peninsula War, and the Battle of Waterloo, where this regiment was awarded the title *Grenadier Guards* for their courage. He became landlord of the Ram Inn in Eastgate Street in Bury St. Edmunds (now demolished), and requested that his coffin be born to his grave by six fellow Waterloo veterans. His memorial stands northwest of the Shire Hall in the Great Churchyard in Bury St. Edmunds. The epitaph reads:

> A husband, father, comrade friend sincere.
> A British soldier brave lies buried here,
> In Spain and Flushing and at Waterloo,
> He fought to guard our country from the foe;
> His comrade Britons who survive him say,
> He acted nobly on that glorious day.

The Grenadier Guards Association had the headstone cleaned and the inscription re-cut on the reverse, after which it was rededicated at a special service.

Lieutenant General Sir Henry Edward Bunbury, the seventh baronet of Great Barton, participated in the Helder Campaign of 1799 and the 1806 expedition to

Naples. As undersecretary of state for war, Sir Henry informed Napoleon of the decision to exile him to St. Helena, leading Napoleon to utter a dramatic speech that death was preferable to this unworthy punishment. Sir Henry was among the first English landowners to establish allotments for their tenants. The Bunbury family burial plot is a walled-off enclosure in the northeast corner of Great Barton churchyard.

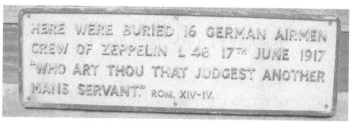

On 17 June 1917 the Zeppelin L48 flew over England, dropping bombs on villages north of Ipswich. Over Theberton it was attacked by three British aeroplanes: catching fire it crashed onto the fields below in a flaming inferno. Remarkably, three of the nineteen crew survived, the only German airmen to survive such a crash over the British Isles during the First World War. The dead crew members received a military funeral with full honours in the extension cemetery on the opposite side of the road from Theberton church. A plaque marking their grave, with a quote from Paul's Epistle to the Romans, was paid for by officers of the Royal Flying Corps. For several years a local war veteran tended the graves, while wreathes were left there every June. In 1966 the remains of Zeppelin crews shot down over Britain were transferred to the German War Cemetery at Cannock Chase in Staffordshire, but this plaque can still be seen in the extension churchyard at Theberton.

Herbert John Leslie Barefoot (who normally used the name Leslie) served in the Royal Army Medical Corps during the First World War. He formed an architectural partnership with Henry Munro Cautley in Ipswich (see page 24), where he designed

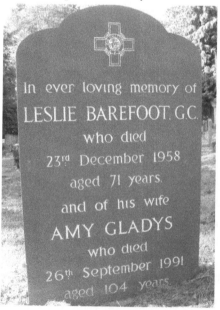

'The Thoroughfare', a remarkably pleasing example of mock Tudor building. In the Second World War he led a bomb disposal unit. On 1 September 1940 unexploded bombs fell on the railway near Ipswich, it was thought these would take a week to defuse, his company defused them in twelve hours. His operations provided valuable examples and techniques for other bomb disposal groups. He was awarded the George Cross for his bravery and example in bomb disposal, the first army officer to receive this honour. His wife presented his George Cross to the Imperial War Museum on her hundredth birthday. His gravestone stands near the Belvedere Road entrance of the Ipswich New Cemetery (plot XJ).

Vladimir Peniakoff, better known as 'Popski' was born in Belgium to a Russian émigré family of partial Jewish extraction. He ran a factory in Egypt, spending his spare time exploring the Sahara Desert and learning Arabic. Considered too old for active military service at the start of the Second World War, by charm and persistence he obtained a commission with the Libyan Arab force, a little regarded native unit. To his superiors' amazement he organised effective sabotage missions on Erwin Rommel's fuel supplies. In 1942 he formed a 23 man platoon, 'Number One Demolition Squadron' (the British army's smallest independent unit) to continue sabotage and reconnaissance. A military signaller shortened his name to 'Popski', a general facetiously called the platoon 'Popski's Private Army', and

the name stuck. The unit performed remarkable exploits in North Africa and Italy. 'Popski' heard that an allied general intended to shell the Basilica of Sant'Apollinare in Ravenna in Italy, a masterpiece of early Christian architecture, believing German soldiers had occupied the tower. Concerned by this, he made his way through enemy lines to find the basilica unoccupied, saving it from destruction. Losing his right hand to a shell at the end of the war, 'Popski' was awarded the Military Cross and the Distinguished Service Order. His war memoirs, *Popski's Private Army*, was a bestseller. He married Pamela Firth, a native of Suffolk: they moved to Wixoe, where he is buried in the churchyard. The astrolabe on the gravestone was his platoon's badge, chosen because he owned a boat of that name, and his men used the stars to find their way across the Sahara.

Denise Dufournier was a lawyer in Paris. In 1942 she joined the *Comet Line* (*Le Réseau Comète*) a resistance organisation that transported allied airmen trapped in Europe to Gibraltar, from whence they could return to Britain. Captured, she was incarcerated in Ravensbruck Concentration Camp: the book she wrote about her experiences, *La Maison des Mortes*, translated into English as *Ravensbruck: the Women's Camp of Death*, is a standard work on the subject. She was awarded the Croix de Guerre, the Legion d'Honneur, and the Freedom Medal of the U.S.A. Before the war she met James McAdam Clark, who served with the Royal Artillery during the Second World War, receiving the Military Cross. Reunited in 1946, Denise and James married, and had two daughters. James was a diplomat in South America and Europe; he and Denise retired to Aldeburgh, where they

are buried in the churchyard, under a headstone displaying the 'Cross of Lorraine', the badge of the French resistance. The Royal Air Forces Escaping Society placed a metal plaque on the monument in Denise's honour.

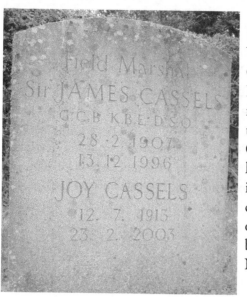

Field Marshall Sir James Cassels led the 51st Highland Division in the Second World War. As commander of the First Commonwealth Division during the Korean War, he won popularity for visiting forward positions. After further service in the Malayan emergency he was appointed Chief of the General Staff (the professional head of the British Army). A physical fitness instructor, he played first class cricket for the combined army team. He spent the last years of his retirement in Barrow, where he was buried in the modern extension cemetery in New Road, east of the parish church.

The Victoria Cross is undoubtedly the most prestigious and romantic of all awards for military heroism. Six Victoria Cross winners have gravestones in Suffolk. Guidebooks recount how Bardwell Church was rebuilt by Sir William de Bardwell, who served in the Hundred Years War. Yet they usually omit to mention Henry Addison's grave, southeast of the church. Born in Bardwell, Henry Addison served with the army in India. During the Indian Mutiny, on 2 January 1859, near Kurrereah, his commanding officer, Lieutenant Willoughby Osborne, was attacked by native troops. Henry Addison covered Lieutenant Osborne and fought off the attackers: in so doing his left leg was badly wounded and had to be amputated above the knee. Retiring from the army with medals for long service and good conduct, he was awarded the Victoria Cross for outstanding bravery and self-sacrifice in saving his commanding officer. Because of his artificial leg, after Queen Victoria presented him with the medal he was allowed to break court protocol and turn his back on her as he withdrew. Seeing his difficulty in walking the Queen had an artificial leg made for him at her own expense.

Samuel Harvey was a private in the York and Lancaster Regiment. On 29 September 1915, when he was 34, his regiment was under attack in the 'Big Willie' trench on the Western Front. His unit was running out of artillery shells, so he volunteered to fetch some. As the communication trench was blocked he repeatedly ran across open ground under intense fire, to bring thirty boxes of shells, sufficient to repel the attacking force, before being disabled by a head wound. He was awarded the Victoria Cross, the French Legion d'Honneur and the Russian Cross of the Order of St. George. Falling into poverty he lost his Victoria Cross (it is one of the few whose whereabouts are unknown). When he died in Stow Lodge Hospital in Stowmarket, aged 79, his only possessions were his miniature medal group; he was buried in Ipswich Old Cemetery (plot X). When Michael Brown, a historian of the First World War, found that Samuel had no gravestone, he contacted the Suffolk branch of the Western Front Association, who raised funds to provide this headstone, which was dedicated on 29 September 2000, the anniversary of the day Samuel won his Victoria Cross.

Thomas Crisp was a member of a Lowestoft maritime family. At 26 he became skipper of the fishing ketch *George Borrow*. At the outbreak of the First World War he was considered ineligible for military service, being nearly 40 years old and engaged in an industry that was vital to ensuring Britain's food supply. Fishing vessels were prime targets of the German 'U Boat' campaign to destroy British shipping: the *George Borrow* was sunk in 1915. The Royal Navy countered U-boats with armed decoy vessels such as 'Q Ships', some fishing vessels were fitted with concealed armaments. Thomas became skipper of the armed fishing smack *I'll Try*. On 1 February 1917 *I'll Try* and

another armed smack, *The Boy Alfred*, repelled two German submarines. Thomas was awarded the Distinguished Service Cross, but declined an offer to command a Q-ship as his wife was terminally ill. On 15 August 1917 *I'll Try* and *Boy Alfred*, re-named *Nelson* and *Ethel And Millie* exchanged fire with a powerful U-boat. The *Nelson* was holed below the waterline. Another shell blew Thomas's legs off. Fatally wounded, but conscious, Thomas continued to command the *Nelson*, destroying confidential documents, and attaching a rescue plea to *Red Cock*, a carrier pigeon kept for such emergencies. Insisting on remaining on board ship, he died as his crew disembarked in a lifeboat. The *Ethel And Millie* was sunk. The U-boat captured her crew. Nothing more was heard of them and their fate remains a mystery. Red Cock reached Lowestoft, and the *Nelson*'s crew were rescued by the fishery protection vessel *The Dryad*. Thomas was awarded a posthumous Victoria Cross for courage in his final, fatal combat. He is commemorated by Tom Crisp Way in Lowestoft. His wife's gravestone, honouring him too, is in Lowestoft Cemetery, between Normanston Drive and Rotterdam Road (plot F, grave 90).

Rawdon Hume Middleton, a 27 year old Australian stationed at R.A.F. Mildenhall, commanded a Stirling I bomber in a raid over Turin on 28th November 1942. Coming under anti-aircraft fire he received shrapnel wounds and lost one eye. Despite incredible pain, and the knowledge that he was fatally wounded, he was determined to return his crew to Britain and reached the coast with five minutes of fuel reserves. Five of the crew then parachuted to safety. Two others stayed with him until ordered to bail out (sadly they did not survive). Rather than risk harming people by crash landing his plane on land, he flew over the ocean until fuel ran out and the aeroplane plummeted into the sea. His posthumous Victoria Cross citation read 'his devotion to duty in the face of overwhelming odds is unsurpassed in the annals of the Royal Air Force'. His body was washed ashore next February and buried in the Commonwealth War Graves Commission cemetery beside St. John's Church in Beck Row, with 72 other airmen from R.A.F. Mildenhall who lost their lives during the Second World War.

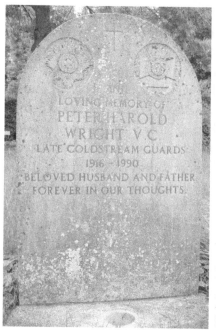

Peter Harold Wright was born in Mettingham. During the Second World War he fought in North Africa and Italy, rising to the rank of Sergeant Major. In the attack on Salerno on 25 September 1943 his company came under heavy machine gun and artillery fire. As the officers were killed Peter Harold Wright took command and led his company against three machine gun posts: repelled by heavy fire, he withdrew, then led a second assault to take the position. His company held off a German counter-attack, during which he returned through enemy fire to bring ammunition. He was recommended for the Distinguished Conduct Medal, but George VI asked for this to be replaced by the Victoria Cross (the only time a monarch has done so). Returning to his native Suffolk, he is buried in Ashbocking Churchyard.

Cavendish village green is a beautiful and widely photographed location. Few people are aware that the village cemetery on the northwest of this congenial spot contains the grave of two of the twentieth century's most remarkable Britons: Leonard Cheshire and Sue Ryder. Geoffrey Leonard Cheshire, to use his full name, graduated from Oxford at the outbreak of the Second World War, when he joined the R.A.F. Enlisting in Bomber Command he developed a 'master bomber' technique, when one plane (often his own) flew at a low altitude as a marker for other aircraft. The R.A.F.'s youngest group captain, he received the Victoria Cross for a continual record of outstanding service. After his hundredth mission Leonard Cheshire became a staff liaison officer to the U.S.A. After acting as an official observer when an atom bomb was dropped on Nagasaki he decided to devote his life to promoting peace. He set up a 'Leonard Cheshire Home' for ex-servicemen and people suffering from disabilities.

Margaret Susan ('Sue') Ryder joined the First Aid Nursing Yeomanry ('F.A.N.Y.'), at the start of the Second World War. A driver and radio operator for Special Operations Executive, she was impressed by the Polish servicemen she met. After the war she worked with Red Cross relief units. Encountering concentration camp survivors and 'displaced persons', she took personal initiatives to help them regain a semblance of normal life. Her family had owned land in south-west Suffolk, and she established 'the Sue Ryder Foundation', a home for disabled people, in a family property at Cavendish.

Other 'Cheshire Homes' and 'Sue Ryder Homes' followed in Britain and overseas. Leonard Cheshire and Sue Ryder met in 1955 and travelled to Dehradun in India to establish the *Raphael Centre*, a medical relief establishment. Marrying in 1959, they moved into a flat in the Sue Ryder Home in Cavendish, from where they supervised the organisations they had created. The only married couple to receive separate peerages for their distinguished careers, as Baroness Ryder of Warsaw (in tribute to the Polish people) and Baron Cheshire of Woodhall, they were buried under an inconspicuous headstone, which pays an amazingly short tribute to their achievements.

Leonard Cheshire Disability is now one of the world's most important organisations working to help people with disabilities; *Sue Ryder* provides assistance for people with life-changing illnesses across England, Eastern Europe and Africa; *The Lady Ryder of Warsaw Memorial Trust* operates to relieve poverty and disease and to assist refugees; while *The Ryder-Cheshire Foundation* works to rehabilitate the disabled and eradicate tuberculosis. Leonard Cheshire and Sue Ryder showed that if people are ready to work selflessly, something positive can be reclaimed from the horrors of warfare.

Residents of the Sue Ryder Home at Cavendish are buried in the village's extension cemetery. Wincenty Zarembski, a Colonel in the Polish army, was awarded the Virtuti Militari, the Polish army's highest award, in the Polish-Soviet War of 1919-21. During the Second World War he worked for the Resistance in Nazi occupied France, running a radio station that passed information to the allies and resistance movements. The British Army awarded him the Distinguished Service Order (D.S.O.). He was buried next to Leonard Cheshire: this is the only place where winners of the Victoria Cross and the D.S.O. are buried beside each other.

Kazimierz Gruszcynski, a Polish army officer, escaped from a prisoner of war camp to join the Polish Resistance. Recaptured, he was sent to Maydanek Concentration Camp, from which he escaped by swimming under the ice on a frozen lake. The Resistance gave him a false identity, and he became a local government official, using the post to pass on information about the Nazis. When he was identified he was sent to Auschwitz, then Buchenwald, before being moved to the slave labour camp at Mittelbau Dora. Ultimately he and 140 other inmates of Dora endured a hellish ten day journey in a cattle truck to Bergen Belsen. The Allied armies liberated Belsen a few weeks later. Given some bread, Kazimierz had the foresight to suck it: like most inmates of Belsen his ordeal had so weakened his system that ingesting solid food would have killed him. He lived with fellow refugees in a makeshift settlement on the site of a concentration camp before Sue Ryder found him a home in Cavendish.

Sofia Grabowska (or Sofia Wyszynska, as she was called after her second marriage) was a nurse in Poland. Aged 53 at the start of the Second World War, she joined the Resistance with members of her family. After participating in the 1944 Warsaw Uprising she, her brother and her pregnant sister-in-law were taken to Mauthausen, where her brother and new-born nephew died of typhus and starvation, and her sister-in-law was killed undergoing medical experiments. Transported to Ravensbruck, on many occasions Sofia narrowly missed being selected for execution, the gas chamber or medical experimentation. When she was critically ill with typhus the Soviet army liberated Ravensbruck. Sue Ryder gave Sofia a room overlooking the garden in her home at Cavendish.

Kazimierz Gruszcynski and Sofia Grabowska lived through atrocities of war and horror beyond imagination. In the work of Sue Ryder and Leonard Cheshire they saw something of the more positive side of humanity and the beauty of peace. Their stories are not just history, but a reminder to all people to be ready to resist evil and hatred, and be aware of the power of compassion.

Edward Rotheram was first officer of the *Culloden* at the Third Battle of Ushant in 1794 (commonly known as 'the glorious first of June'). At the Battle of Trafalgar he was Vice-Admiral Collingwood's flag-captain on the *Royal Sovereign*. Collingwood was dismissive of his abilities and they did not get on very well. Nevertheless, he was awarded a gold medal and a sword of honour for his service, and was placed in command of the *Bellerophon*, whose captain had been killed in the battle. Two years later his naval career was effectively terminated after he was court-martialled for unacceptable conduct to his junior officers and chaplain. For the rest of his life he agitated for recognition of his services, which he felt were unappreciated. He died visiting an acquaintance at Bildeston and was buried in the churchyard. Sixty years later he received some recognition when this marble memorial was placed over his grave.

John Green, an Orford mariner, took part in Captain Parry's Arctic expedition of 1819-20 which aimed to find the 'North West Passage', a navigable route around the north coast of America, a goal of explorers since the sixteenth century. The expedition established that this route existed, but was so ice-bound that it was impractical to navigate. Returning to Orford, John Green became a ship's master. He lived to 94, the longest surviving member of Parry's expedition. His memorial in Orford churchyard, built to resemble an arctic cairn, displays a representation of Captain Parry's ship, *The Hecla*.

Among Suffolk's many distinguished lifeboatmen, Joshua Chard was the only one to be known as 'the Suffolk hero'. Born in Dorset, at three he was sent to Aldringham where he was brought up by an aunt. Although apprenticed to a carpenter, he bought a boat and made a living as a sailor at Thorpe, the fishing village which was later developed as Thorpeness. A pilot who guided vessels into Suffolk harbours, when the Thorpe lifeboat was instituted he became the coxswain. (During the nineteenth century lifeboat crews rowed to ships in distress, often through terrible storms.) He kept a diary of his exploits: it would be interesting to know if this survives. Suffolk author Ernest Read Cooper's *Storm Warriors of the Suffolk Coast* (1937) and the *Ipswich Journal* of 17 July 1869 describe seven rescues when he saved over thirty lives. The *Ipswich Journal* of 21 May 1870 records a county wide subscription to buy him a new lifeboat, appropriately called the *Rescue*. On 21 December 1875 he drowned when returning from piloting a steamboat to Gravesend. He is buried in Aldringham churchyard, under this cross (described in the *Ipswich Journal* of 21 August 1877), south of the church. His name is decipherable, but an inscription naming him 'the Suffolk hero' has worn away.

Pakefield lifeboat station has been lost to coastal erosion, but the headstones of two of its coxswains can be seen in Pakefield churchyard. Nathaniel Colby was awarded R.N.L.I. silver medals for leading the rescue of the crews of the *Zemira* (when his crew all received bronze medals); and the *Shamrock*. He received £38 from the French government for saving the crew of *Le Jeune Mathilde*. George Meek Warford succeeded Nathaniel Colby as coxswain, holding the post for 33 years. Physically big and strong he was reserved in conversation, known locally as 'mute' because he might go for several days without speaking. Recipient of three R.N.L.I. silver medals, he was also in charge of the Clifton Road volunteer firemen in the adjoining village of Kirkley. His coffin was borne to the grave by eight other lifeboat coxswains. Between themselves they saved over 400 lives.

William Mann's gravestone in Aldeburgh churchyard displays the anchor of hope and the cross of faith. He was a crew member of the Aldeburgh lifeboat for forty years, and second coxswain for eighteen of these. His obituary in the *Aldeburgh and Saxmundham Times* of October 1903 says he helped save the crews of three foreign ships: the *Venscapen*; the *Antares* and the *Winnifred* for which he received a gratuity from the Russian government; a silver watch from the Kaiser and a medal from the King of Norway.

Robert Hook stood 6 feet 3 inches high. Originally a fisherman, he joined the Lowestoft lifeboat as a teenager, becoming coxswain at 25. Twice awarded the R.N.L.I. silver medal, he helped save over 600 lives. Once he led a rescue, unaware that the crew had already rowed to safety in their own ship's lifeboat. Finding the ship's dog and cat on board, he took them back to land. In later years he ran the *Fisherman's Arms* pub in Lowestoft. His grave, recently restored, stands in Lowestoft Public Cemetery, between Rotterdam Road and Normanston Drive (plot 11, grave 319).

Britain entered the First World War on 4 August 1914 when it declared war on Germany. That day the S.S. *Koningen Luise* laid mines in the Thames. On 5 August a Royal Naval task force pursued her, opening fire and killing some of the crew. The commander ordered that she be scuttled to prevent her falling into British hands: the task force took the German crew into custody. The following morning H.M.S. *Amphion*, from the British task force, struck a mine laid by the *Koningen Luise*, causing fatalities among the crew and captives. Some were laid to rest in Shotley churchyard: the first casualties of the War buried on British soil.

Arthur Young was one of the most important figures of the Agricultural Revolution. The son of the Rector of Bradfield Combust, he farmed there, but spent more time travelling around Britain to investigate new advances in agriculture. He wrote books and edited a journal, *Annals of Agriculture*, showing how these could be put into practice. When the Board of Agriculture was established Arthur Young was its first Secretary: although he went blind in later life, he conscientiously continued to perform his duties. He did more than anybody else to promote, publicise and disseminate information about new farming methods, which ensured that Britain fed her population and armies during the French Revolutionary and Napoleonic Wars. He was indirectly responsible for originating the 'Suffolk Black Faced' sheep. East Anglian farmers kept 'Norfolk Horn' sheep: Arthur acquired a hornless 'Southdown' ram from Sussex, who got loose among a herd of Norfolk horn ewes and impregnated twelve before he was caught! The resulting lambs were thought to be of such high quality that breeding followed. Arthur Young's memorial in Bradfield Combust churchyard includes the inscriptions 'in agriculture and political economy pre-eminent' and

> Let every true patriot shed a tear
> For genius talents worth lie buried here.

Richard Garrett (I) was the progenitor of one of Suffolk's most dynamic and enterprising families. In 1778 he moved from Woodbridge, where his family were bladesmiths, to Leiston, where he ran a forge, which grew to employ ten men. He was buried in Leiston churchyard in 1839 beside his wife, Elizabeth Garrett (nee Newson).

Richard I's son, Richard Garrett (II), took over the forge, which grew under his management. This memorial in Leiston churchyard was erected on his death in 1837. Topped by a cast iron urn from the Leiston works, it symbolised the family's growing prosperity and importance, with spaces for later generations. (Richard I may have been omitted as he outlived his son.) (See *A History of Suffolk Gravestones* page 72.)

Richard II's son, Richard Garrett III, turned 'Richard Garrett and Sons' into one of Britain's leading manufacturers of agricultural equipment, exporting products worldwide. As a participant in the Great Exhibition of 1851 Richard saw U.S. exhibitors using 'assembly line' methods to make pistols. Inspired by this he built the 'Long Shop' at Leiston, where agricultural machines could be constructed piece by piece, the world's first production line factory. (A rare example of an Englishman taking advantage of U.S. enterprise!) By his death, aged only 59, he employed 600 men, and had overseen

Leiston's growth from a village into a town. Richard Garrett III bought Carlton Hall: he was buried under this imposing sarcophagus in Carlton churchyard. An inscription on the side commemorates his older son, Richard Garrett IV, who continued to run the Leiston works, while becoming a gentleman farmer and breeder of Suffolk Punch horses.

On Richard Garrett IV's death, management of the Leiston factory passed to his brother Frank. While Frank Garrett resisted trade unionism, he maintained a paternalist attitude to his workforce: with the demands of the First World War he eventually employed over 1,500 people.

Frank Garrett's son, Frank Garrett (II), was an active member of the Volunteers (army reservists) and the Territorial Army. Although aged 45 at the start of the First World War he accompanied his men to France, but the strain of military service caused a nervous breakdown and he was invalided out of the forces. After the War Frank pooled his resources with eleven other engineering companies to form 'A.G.E.' (Amalgamated and General Engineers), a venture which proved disastrous to all participants. Unable to survive the Slump, 'Richard Garrett and Sons' closed in 1932. Frank remained active in local government, receiving a knighthood for his services in this area. The Garretts owned a house at Aldringham, and had a family plot in Aldringham churchyard where Frank I and II are buried. The engineering works was bought and revived by Beyer, Peacock and Co.; it continued as part of larger combines until its final closure in January 1981. The factory is now *The Long Shop Museum*, a brilliant attraction which should be visited by anybody with an interest in Suffolk's history or Britain's industrial heritage.

Richard Garrett III's younger brother, Newson Garrett, bought a corn and coal merchants at Snape which he developed into one of England's largest malting businesses. Living in Alde House in Aldeburgh, he played an important role in the town's Victorian expansion, designing and building Brudenell Terrace, Park Road and the Jubilee Hall. Richard Garrett III and Newson married sisters; despite this they are said to have been bitter rivals, but tales of their hostility may have been exaggerated, as they co-operated to establish a railway line that linked Aldeburgh and Leiston to the national rail network. Newson Garrett was buried in a family vault beside Aldeburgh church, but his most stupendous monument must be Snape Maltings, which he designed. One of Britain's largest (and most beautiful) Victorian industrial buildings, this is now a concert hall and arts centre, hosting the Aldeburgh Festival.

Newson's daughter, Elizabeth Garrett, was the first Englishwoman to become a doctor. As women were not allowed to study medicine at English universities, she learned French to take a medical degree in Paris, after which she opened the first British hospital to only employ female staff. Marrying James Anderson, a shipping entrepreneur, she took the name Elizabeth Garrett Anderson. She retired to Aldeburgh. As an early leader of the movement for women's suffrage, she helped advance the cause when she was elected mayor of Aldeburgh, the first female mayor of an English town. She was buried in her father's family vault in Aldeburgh churchyard.

At the end of the eighteenth century James Smyth opened a wheelwright's shop in Peasenhall, where he designed 'the Suffolk Drill', a horse drawn seed planting machine. He is buried in a stone chest tomb in Peasenhall churchyard (foreground). His son, James Smyth (Junior) expanded 'Smyth's of Peasenhall', opening a second factory at Witham in Essex and a depot in Paris to exploit the Continental market. Eventually James Smyth (Junior) employed 120 men in Peasenhall, establishing a benefit society for his workers and founding a Mechanics' Institute in the village. He is commemorated by the obelisk, (background).

James Josiah Smyth, James (Junior)'s son, was sent to Germany to study technology there. He continued to run the company: well-travelled in Europe, he liked Switzerland, and paid for Peasenhall's Swiss style village hall. He was buried in the modern cemetery in Hackney Road at the west end of Peasenhall. As he had no children 'Smyth's of Peasenhall' was taken over by a Thirtle family, and operated until 1967. Parts of the factory remain beside the churchyard, overlooking the graves of the company's pioneers.

John Childs came to Bungay as an apprentice at a printing works. Marrying his master's daughter, he became a partner in the business, then the proprietor. An innovator of low cost quality publishing, his *Imperial Edition of Standard Authors* produced classic literature for a wide readership. By printing cheap price Bibles he helped end the state-controlled right to print the Bible in England. A member of the Congregational Church and advocate

of Parliamentary reform, he supported campaigns to raise the status of Nonconformists, while inviting many leading radicals to Bungay. His refusal to pay rates to the Church of England led to a brief imprisonment, leading his admirers to call him 'the Bungay martyr' and his opponents to label him 'the spoilt child'. John Childs is buried in front of the Congregational Church in Upper Olland Street in Bungay. The company he developed was bought by Clay, Son and Taylor; as 'Clay's' it is Britain's largest printing works, producing over 100 million volumes a year, including the *Harry Potter* books.

John Whitmore was born in Wickham Market. His millwright father died when he was eleven; he later took over his late father's business premises and built Buttrum's Mill at Woodbridge. In 1868 he formed 'Whitmore and Binyon' in partnership with George Binyon, a Lancashire Quaker, which became a nationally known company, employing 200 men, with an office in London. Its products included 'assembly kit' windmills that could be shipped abroad and fitted together on arrival. John Whitmore's memorial in Wickham Market churchyard suggests the honour in which 'Whitmore and Binyon' was held, but it collapsed in 1901, after 'cash flow' problems. Whitmore and Binyon engines are displayed at the Museum of East Anglian Life at Stowmarket.

It is impossible to write about the history of Haverhill without mentioning the Gurteen family. Daniel Gurteen (I) was a clothier in Haverhill, supplying raw material to local workers, then collecting and selling the finished products. In 1784 he formed a company with £1,000 capital that became the largest employer in the area. The Gurteens were Congregationalists; his gravestone stands behind the Congregational Church in Hamlet Road, Haverhill. The epitaph is a poem by William Cowper, which became a hymn.

Daniel Gurteen (I)'s son, Daniel Gurteen II, developed the family business; his son, Daniel Gurteen (III) (known in the family as Daniel Gurteen Senior) turned it into one of East Anglia's largest clothing manufacturers. Daniel Gurteen III opened the Chauntry Mill Factory in Haverhill in 1856, he eventually employed 3,000 people. Haverhill was known for the manufacture of 'drabbet' a hard wearing linen/cotton mix, ideal for agricultural workers' smocks: the Gurteen family monopolised production of these. A magistrate and active figure in local government, Daniel III financed the building of Haverhill's ostentatious Town Hall (now an excellent arts and local history centre) and Congregational Church (the town's largest public building). In 1886 he handed the business to his son, Daniel Gurteen (IV, known in the family as Daniel Gurteen Junior) who continued to play an important role in the family business and local government, founding the Haverhill Choral Society, which still functions. Dying within a year of each other, in 1894 and 1895, Daniel Senior and Junior were buried under this elaborate structure in Haverhill town cemetery in Withersfield Road. Gurteens still operates from the Chauntry Mill Factory, under the management of Christopher Gurteen, a descendant of Daniel (I): the U.K. record for the longest direct management of a manufacturing company by the same family.

Joseph Tetley was born in Bradford in 1811; at eleven he began selling goods on horseback with his brother Edward. Before they were thirty they had established their own business, tea being their most popular commodity. They became London tea merchants, in 1865 Joseph separated from Edward to form 'Joseph Tetley and Co.', one of the world's largest tea companies. His daughter Sarah married George Jones, a doctor in Framlingham (they took the surname 'Tetley-Jones'). Joseph retired to Broadwater House in Framlingham; in 1899 he was buried under a cross in the cemetery in Fore Street in Framlingham. The smaller stone in the foreground commemorates George and Sarah's son, William Tetley-Jones, a later head of the company. William married

Grizeal, sister of Field Marshall Ironside. Their son, given the exotic name Tetley Ironside Tetley-Jones, performed the immortal service of introducing the teabag to Britain in 1953. Tetley Ironside Tetley-Jones's wife, Mary, is commemorated by the stone before Edward's memorial.

In about 1790 William Churchman opened a tobacconist's shop in Ipswich. His son, another William, opened a cigarette factory, and became a town councillor. William (II)'s son, Henry Charles Churchman, established one of England's largest cigarette factories in Portman Road. William Churchman (II) and Henry Charles Churchman's gravestones stand close together in Ipswich Old Cemetery (plot J).

Henry Charles Churchman had two sons, William Alfred and Arthur Charles, from whom the firm took the name 'W. A. and A. C. Churchman'. Early in the twentieth century William and Arthur pooled resources with other British tobacco companies to form the 'Imperial Tobacco Company', and combat the aggressive 'American Tobacco Company'. (The trade war ended with a truce, when both companies agreed to respect each other's business spheres.) A leading member of the First Volunteer Battalion of the Suffolk Regiment William was created a baronet for services to the British army during the First World War. Although William lived at Melton Lodge in Woodbridge he was buried in the churchyard of St. Peter and St. Paul's church at Felixstowe in 1947. He and Arthur had no sons, so the

Churchman dynasty came to an end after their death, but the brand name 'Churchman's' continued in use until 1972. While the controversies surrounding smoking cannot be discussed here it might be noted that scientists only began to seriously consider its health implications in the 1930's. The Portman Road factory closed in 1992 and has been converted into offices. Perhaps prompted by the family name, Churchman's produced cigarette cards showing Suffolk churches.

James Maconochie became a fish merchant in Lowestoft aged 21, in partnership with his brother Archibald. 'Maconochie Brothers' opened a shop in Belvedere Road, followed by factories in Clapham Road and Raglan Street, producing cured fish, potted meat and jam. In 1885 James and Archibald won the contract to supply rations to the British army, by then Maconochie Brothers was one of the world's leading manufacturers of processed foods. James died at the early age of 42 and was buried under this impressive art deco memorial in Lowestoft public cemetery in Normanston Drive (plot 3, grave 90). By then Maconochie Brothers had an annual turnover of £250,000, had business premises in Scotland and London (giving its name to Maconochie Wharf on the Thames). The company later made 'Pan Yan' pickle. Maconochie Brothers closed its Lowestoft operations in 1926; it merged into the Rowntree Macintosh group in 1967. The Maconochie Brothers factory gives its name to Maconochie Way in Lowestoft, yet probably deserves greater appreciation for its role in the town's industrial development.

The working man's struggle for recognition, fair wages and reasonable working conditions must always be remembered. It is therefore appropriate that a trade unionist's gravestone should receive some appreciation. Horace Rampling was a bricklayer. Between 1881 and 1901 the censuses show him living in Navarre Street in Ipswich with his wife, Elizabeth, and children. He was an early Labour Party Councillor, for St. Margaret's Ward in Ipswich, and a member of the council of the Operative Bricklayer's Society, which had 40,000 members at the time (since merged into the Union of Construction, Allied Trades and Technicians (U.C.A.T.T.). The *East Anglian Daily Times* of 14 February 1911 says that, after taking the train to Bentley, where he was helping to build a farm for the Co-Operative Society, he misguidedly walked across the railway lines, rather than the bridge, and was struck by a train. His obituary said 'he was always regarded as a careful and painstaking official, was fearless and outspoken in the advancement of the views he held, and was greatly respected by all with whom he came into contact'. His gravestone, in Ipswich Old Cemetery (plot X) shows emblems of the Operative Bricklayer's Society.

'The smugglers' grave' stands in Tunstall churchyard. In June 1778 smugglers unloaded 300 barrels of gin at Sizewell Gap, a favoured spot for landing contraband, concealing these in a dug-out on Coldfair Green, near Leiston. When the smugglers returned two of them, Robert Debney and William Cooper, eagerly jumped into the dug-out, but failed to come out: they had been suffocated by alcohol fumes. Leaving the bodies, the smugglers carried the gin to the *Parrot* Inn at Aldringham, when excisemen arrived, seized the barrels, and took them to Saxmundham, where they were publicly broken and their contents poured into the ground. Robert Debney and William Cooper's fathers were a farmer and a miller at Tunstall. Their epitaph is sympathetic: perhaps it was thought they deserved Christian compassion, or their families did not regard them as disreputable.

All you dear friends that look upon this stone
Oh think how quickly both their lives were gone
Neither age nor sickness brought them to decay
Death quickly took their strength and life away
Both in the prime of life they lost their breath
And on a sudden were cast down by death
A cruel death that could no longer spare
A loving husband, nor a child most dear
The loss is great to those they left behind
But they through Christ 'tis hoped true joy will find.

Henry Scarle's gravestone, in the churchyard of Holy Trinity church in Bungay, is the only headstone in Suffolk to identify a person as a murder victim. His career was linked with the fortunes of Matthias Kerrison (whose memorial stands inside the church), a local entrepreneur who became one of Britain's first 'millionaires' after buying the Waveney navigation in 1784. This was run incompetently, and theft from vessels was rife. Matthias Kerrison announced his intention to run the navigation efficiently. Hearing of this, Henry Scarle informed on three robbers who had stolen grain from his boat. The robbers attacked Henry Scarle, beating him so badly that he died. Matthias Kerrison publicised the horror of the murder, exhibiting the body in the *Three Tuns* in Bungay (charging a penny to see it). The assailants were tried: one turned 'king's evidence' (testifying in return for immunity from prosecution) and the other two were hanged. Matthias Kerrison used this as a starting point for enforcing new standards on the Waveney navigation, erecting this gravestone at his own expense to encourage honesty.

Sarah Lloyd was a servant to Sarah Syer, a widow in Hadleigh. She began a liaison with Joseph Clarke, who persuaded her to help him burgle Mrs. Syer's house. To cover their tracks they set fires in the house. Neighbours saw the flames, roused Mrs Syer and extinguished the fires. Apprehended separately from Joseph, Sarah was found with money and jewellery worth ten pounds. Sarah and Joseph were tried at Bury St. Edmunds, but, while Joseph instigated the crime and took advantage of Sarah, only Sarah was found guilty, as she was carrying the stolen goods. Theft of goods worth over twenty shillings was a capital offence: although courts did not always enforce the maximum penalty in such cases (especially with women), the judge sentenced her to death as she had broken a position of trust and put her mistress's life at risk by lighting fires in the house. Capel Lofft, a landowner at Troston and a magistrate, campaigned for Sarah's reprieve, writing to government officials

arguing for leniency and organising a petition on her behalf, but to no avail, he was struck off the list of magistrates after speaking about the injustice of the case at the execution. A memorial on the Charnel House in the Great Churchyard in Bury St. Edmunds describes Sarah's death as 'just but ignominious'. While Joseph Clarke is not named it is implied he was the true villain: the reader must decide the fairness of these statements for themself. The *Bury Post* of 2 April 1806 reported that Joseph Clarke joined the army (perhaps being no longer welcome in Suffolk) and died in the West Indies: in his last days he admitted responsibility for the crime.

John Orridge became governor of Bury St. Edmunds gaol in 1798, where he introduced medical care and religious services. In 1804 he supervised the construction of a prison on Sicklesmere Road, built to impressive new standards. Here he initiated education and creative employment, setting up a garden for the prisoners to cultivate. Rather more controversially he was the first prison governor to use the *Treadmill*, a perpetual roller for prisoners to walk on, opinions vary as to whether this was exercise, therapy or torture. Bury Gaol became internationally famous: the Tsar of Russia asked John Orridge for information on prison design and management. John Orridge was gaoler to Sarah Lloyd (see above) whom he treated with some sympathy. The most notorious prisoner to pass through Bury Gaol during his (or any other governor's) term of office was William Corder, who shot Maria Marten in the *Red Barn Murder* at Polstead in 1828: John Orridge helped persuade Corder to make a final confession on the night before the execution, which brought 10,000 people to Bury. After John Orridge's death it was found that he had ignored government rules on prison management, running the gaol according to his own principles, employing prisoners for his personal service, and profiting from the supply of food and other items to the gaol (such activities were not uncommon in contemporary penal institutions). He was buried to the north of the Shire Hall in the Great Churchyard in Bury St. Edmunds: unfortunately only fragments of his memorial survive.

Only two Suffolk policemen have been murdered while on service. James McFadden was a 27 year old Irishman who had joined the Suffolk constabulary. On 28 July 1848 he saw five men stealing grain from a barn in Gisleham. When he attempted to arrest them one fired a shotgun, seriously wounding him, the gang then fled. P.C. McFadden crawled to a nearby farmhouse: a doctor was called, but he died two days later. P.C. McFadden named William Howell, a Mutford resident, aged 28, and a known criminal, as the man who shot him. William was arrested; his brother Walter and Israel Shipley, aged 21 and 38, were charged as accomplices. They were tried at Bury St. Edmunds, although some witness testimony was doubtful, they were found guilty. William Howell was hanged at Ipswich; Walter and Israel were among the last criminals to be transported to Australia. James McFadden had lodged at Kessingland and is buried in the churchyard there.

Ebenezer Tye was a 24 year old policeman at Halesworth. On 25 November 1862 he tried to arrest John Ducker for theft and poaching. Although aged 63 John Ducker was exceptionally strong and resisted, knocking P.C. Tye out so he fell face first into a nearby stream. John Ducker left P.C. Tye to drown. Tried for murder and found guilty, John Ducker was the last person in Suffolk to be publicly hanged. Ironically, it is unclear if John Ducker was engaged in criminal activity, so had he not resisted arrest he might have been released without charge. Had P.C. Tye fallen in a different direction, or had John Ducker pulled P.C. Tye's head from the stream he would only have been tried for assault and resisting arrest. P.C. Tye was buried in the public cemetery in Holton Road in Halesworth, under a headstone honouring his death 'in the performance of his duty'.

William Napthen was head gamekeeper at Elveden Hall. At 10.30pm on 20 December 1850 he and some estate workers gave chase to six poachers. After crossing the parish boundary into Eriswell three poachers turned and fired their rifles: one estate worker received a minor wound, William was more seriously hurt and died next morning. The poachers outran their pursuers. Six agricultural workers from Isleham, a Cambridgeshire village twelve miles west of Elveden, were spotted carrying rifles the same night. They insisted they were hunting small wild birds, which, upsetting as this may seem to modern ornithologists, was a legally and socially permissible pursuit in Victorian rural communities. In court it was established that the night of the murder was foggy, and none of the pursuers clearly saw the poacher's faces, so the agricultural workers were found not guilty. This caused some celebration in Isleham, where they were regarded as popular and law abiding members of the community. William Napthen's gravestone, near 'the cloisters' in Elveden churchyard, displays quotes from 2 Samuel 1:23 and Matthew 10: 28. An area of Elveden is known as Marmansgrave: William George Clarke's *In Breckland Wilds* (1925) records a tradition that 'Marman' was a gamekeeper who was killed by poachers. Was this a folk memory of the murder?

The victims of two other unsolved murders, which were national sensations, and have since been reinvestigated, are buried in Suffolk. A memorial in the cemetery in Hackney Road in Peasenhall bears the inscription 'in affectionate memory of Rose Annie Harsent whose life was cruelly taken on the 1st of June 1902 in her 23rd year'. Rose Harsent was a servant in Providence House in Peasenhall; on Saturday 31 May she received an anonymous letter requesting a meeting that night (the sender was never identified). Next morning she was found in the kitchen of Providence House with her throat cut: medical examination showed she was six months pregnant (amazingly, no effort was made to discover the father's identity). A year previously two village youths claimed they overheard Rose having a salacious conversation with William Gardiner, a

foreman carpenter at Smyth's Agricultural Works (see page 47), who was married with six children. While it was never established if this was true, this made William Gardiner a prime suspect. His wife provided an alibi, but there was nothing beyond her word to support it; on the other hand, while incriminating evidence was produced, there was no irrefutable proof of his guilt. Two nationally reported trials ended with 'hung juries', unable to reach a unanimous decision, and William Gardiner walked free. He and his family left Peasenhall, and disappeared into obscurity.

William Murfitt was a farmer at Risby. On 17 May 1938 he drank a glass of 'health salts' with his breakfast. He immediately felt ill and died within an hour. Forensic tests showed that, in the previous 24 hours, the salts had been laced with a cyanide compound of a sort widely used on farms for pest control. Chief Inspector Leonard Burt (a distinguished member of the Special Branch) and Detective Sergeant Reg Spooner (who later commanded the Flying Squad) investigated the case. William Murfitt had recently dismissed some of his workers, and pursued liaisons with local women. Thus disgruntled employees, participants in previous indiscretions, and his wife could have harboured grudges against him. It was discovered that William and his wife knew some local people with shady pasts. The investigation, with elements of an Agatha Christie thriller, made Risby a popular tourist destination. Suspects were investigated: their testimonies displayed inconsistencies, but there was insufficient evidence to prosecute anybody. William Murfitt was buried on the north side of Risby churchyard, his death a baffling mystery.

In 1980 Edwin Packer, a local historian, published *The Peasenhall Murder*. In 2004 David Williams, a journalist who was a child in Risby at the time of William Murfitt's death, wrote a best-selling book, *Poison Farm*. Both review the evidence and provide plausible cases for the true murderer's identity. Since neither person can now stand trial, the reader is left to decide on their guilt.

Rachel Parsons was the daughter of Sir Charles Parsons, the inventor of the steam turbine. Active on the 'society circuit', she was the founder and first president of the Women's Engineering Society, and a member of London County Council. In 1947, at 62, she bought Branches Park in Cowlinge, after which she is alleged to have undergone a personality change. Turning into a notorious miser, neglecting her appearance, launching foul-mouthed tirades and viciously lashing out with her handbag, she was prosecuted for dangerous driving and failing to repair her tenant's houses, becoming the prime candidate for the role of the 'most hated person in Newmarket'. Paradoxically, while she neglected Branches Park so badly that it later had to be demolished, she lavished money, care and attention on her racehorses. In 1956 she sacked Dennis Pratt, a stableman, to whom she owed two weeks wages. Soon afterwards Dennis Pratt walked into a Cambridge pawnbroker's shop to sell a set of binoculars: the suspicious shop manager called the police. Dennis Pratt broke down and said that he went to ask Rachel Parsons for his wages: she responded with abuse and set about him with her handbag. In fear, anger and self-defence he lashed out, killing her. He then took enough items to cover the money she owed. When the case came to court he was found guilty of manslaughter, rather than murder (it was suggested that he had been provoked) and received a ten year sentence. Rachel Parsons was buried in the public cemetery in Newmarket, which was closed by a police guard on the day of the funeral.

William Sakings's gravestone, by the south porch of Great Livermere church, is one of the best known churchyard memorials in Suffolk. He was falconer to Charles I, Charles II and James II. (His name seems suitable, as there is a Saker falcon.) Mentioned in many Suffolk guidebooks, it is regarded as a source of pride in Great Livermere.

Guy Aylmer was another falconer. He served in the King's Royal Rifle Corps during the First World War and worked as conservator of forests in the Sudan. He noticed that the 'jess', the leather strap tethering the bird's leg to a perch or falconer's glove

presented dangers: if a falcon flew into a hedge or tree the jess could get tangled in the branches. He devised the 'Aylmeri Jess', a brilliantly simple innovation, with a grommet or hole in the tether end, from which the falconer could quickly unleash the falcon, now a widely used falconry accoutrement. The Aylmer family owned Risby Manor: Guy and his wife Beryl (herself a falconer) are buried in Risby churchyard. Their gravestone displays an appropriate quote from the Book of Job. (39:26)

Three notable sportsmen's graves can be seen in the Old and New Cemeteries in Belvedere Road in Ipswich. John Harding's gravestone stands on the west side of the main footpath from the gateway to the cemetery chapels in the Old Cemetery (plot G). The epitaph says he was the captain of Stoke Wanderers Football Team who died in 1884 from an injury received in a match. I have been unable to find any mention of the unfortunate event in the local press. Stoke Wanderers, an amateur football team from Stoke, the area of Ipswich south of the River Orwell, appeared in the sporting pages of the *Ipswich Journal* between 1876 and 1891: Ipswich Town Football Club played their first ever game against Stoke Wanderers in 1878 (Ipswich Town won 6-1).

'Alf Ramsey' (or Sir Alfred Ernest Ramsey, to use his full name) was the manager of the England Football Team who won the World Cup in 1966, often cited as the greatest moment in English footballing history. In his youth he played for Southampton and Tottenham Hotspur, making 29 appearances for England. In 1955 he became manager of Ipswich Town, then in division three (south) of the football league. Alf Ramsey achieved an amazing turnaround in the club's fortunes: Ipswich Town were third division champions in 1957, second division champions in 1961, and first division champions in 1962. He then became manager of the English national team, where he was the intellect behind a spectacular World Cup win, leading to a knighthood. The English team failed to follow this outstanding success, but, during eleven years of Alf Ramsey's management they played 113 games, winning 69 and drawing 27, perhaps their best overall performance. Alf Ramsey spent the last twenty years of his life in retirement in Ipswich. His ahses lie in the cremation plot near the south entrance to Ipswich Old Cemetery. His statue stands outside Ipswich Town Football ground in a road named 'Sir Alf Ramsey Way'.

Prince Alexander Obolensky's career as a rugby player was truly meteoric: bright and brilliant, but sadly burning out after a brief time. Born to a Russian aristocratic family, his parents came to England after the Revolution when he was three years old. (He abandoned the title 'prince' on becoming a British citizen.) At seventeen he made his Rugby League debut for Rosslyn Park and the English national team. At nineteen he gained fame from 'Obolensky's match': a 13-0 victory over the New Zealand 'All-Blacks' when he carried the ball across the field through the opposing team, one of the greatest 'tries' in Rugby history. (England did not beat the 'All Blacks' again until 1973.) Having joined the R.A.F. Volunteer Reserve, he was commissioned into the R.A.F at the start of the Second World War, to be killed when his plane crashed during a training exercise at Martlesham Heath. He was only 24. He was buried in Ipswich New Cemetery (plot XH), in an area set aside for the R.A.F.: five holders of the Distinguished Flying Cross are buried nearby. His exotic foreign origins, the loyalty with which he served his adopted country, and his youthful promise cut tragically short are a romance of British sporting history. In 2009 his niece, Princess Alexandra Obolensky, unveiled his statue in Cromwell Square in Ipswich.

Ronald ('Ron') Greenwood was a professional footballer who became a coach and trainer. As manager of West Ham, who he guided to win the FA Cup and the European Cup Winners' Cup, he nurtured the skills of Bobby Moore, Geoff Hurst and Martin

Peters. In 1977 he became manager of the English national team (for whom he selected the first black player). Five years later England appeared in the 1982 World Cup, the first time they had qualified since 1970, reaching the second round. Ron Greenwood spent his last years in Suffolk, avoiding publicity: at his death neighbours were surprised to discover his identity. He was buried in the cemetery in Newton Road, Sudbury (next to Clive Madgwick, a successful landscape artist).

Newmarket's associations with horse racing make it Suffolk's best known sporting town. Many important figures from this sport are buried here. Elnathan 'Nat' Flatman walked to Newmarket when he was 15 and persuaded a trainer to take him on as an apprentice jockey. In 1840 he was the first person to be awarded the title of 'Champion Jockey' for winning the most races in the season (in this case, fifty) a title he held until 1852. Achieving a reputation for integrity, he did much to raise the sport's standards. He is buried in All Saints' Churchyard.

'Fred' Archer has often been cited as the greatest jockey who ever lived. He was one of the first sporting heroes to become a 'household word', a public figure whose activities were followed by all ranks of society, even those who normally had no interest in horse racing. Born Frederick James Archer, he was apprenticed to Newmarket trainer Mathew ('Matt') Dawson at eleven, winning his first classic race, the Cesarevitch, at fifteen. At seventeen Fred Archer became Champion Jockey after winning 147 races in a season. In the next twelve years he won 2,600 races, including five Derbys. The expression 'Archer's up', used when he seemed guaranteed to win a race, came into common usage, meaning 'nothing can go wrong'. Fred Archer's success was the more remarkable since he stood five foot ten inches, unusually tall for a jockey, his life was characterised by an incessant effort to to keep his weight low: often he only ate a spoonful of food a day. His marriage to Matt Dawson's niece, Helen Rose ('Nellie'), was a public holiday in Newmarket: special trains brought thousands of people to the town to celebrate the occasion, with a banquet on 'The Severals' (an open area northeast of the town). But their first child died after a few hours, and Nellie died after giving birth to their second child. The effect of this, coupled with the physical and psychological stress of a starvation diet, caused Fred Archer to shoot himself on the anniversary of Nellie's death.

A national outburst of mourning followed: Newmarket was crowded with people who came to watch the funeral procession. He was buried in the public cemetery at the southwest end of Newmarket High Street, which was filled with floral tributes: the crowd was uncontrollable and broke through a police guard to fill the cemetery, not to riot, but to express the sadness at the loss of a popular hero. (Matt Dawson, who shared in much of Fred Archer's life, is buried nearby.) Fred Archer's astonishing career scaled the height of success and plumbed the depths of sorrow: it is not surprising that his ghost is said to ride across Newmarket racecourse.

George Archibald was born in San Francisco, he won the Kentucky Derby at 21 and continued with a successful racing career in Germany. After the U.S. entry into the First World War he was interned in Austria, but he was released through diplomatic channels to Spain, where he raced at San Sebastian. Coming to England in 1922 he won the 2,000 guineas, in the next five years he won 180 races and rode for George V. Difficulty maintaining a low weight may have contributed to his early death at the age of 37. His memorial displays the widest selection of horseracing emblems in Newmarket Cemetery.

George Lambton was the second son of the Earl of Durham. Leaving Cambridge University to pursue a horseracing career he became a champion amateur jockey, then a racehorse trainer at Newmarket. He trained the winners of many classic races, most famously *Hyperion*, winner of the 1933 Derby, whose statue stands outside the Jockey Club headquarters in Newmarket. George Lambton exposed the practice of 'doping' horses to win races; his autobiography, *Men and Horses I Have Known*, is a classic of horseracing literature. His memorial in Newmarket Cemetery, which says he led 'a long and glorious life', also records his children: Sybil (whose middle name, 'Diadem', was taken from one of his most successful horses); John, who died in the R.A.F. during the Second World War; and Edward (Teddy), another successful trainer.

Harry Wragg (Harry was his first name) won 13 classic races, including three Derbys: he was Champion Jockey in 1941, at 39, after winning 81 races in a season. He was called 'the head waiter' from his tactic of holding his horse back until late in the race, then pulling ahead to win. After retiring as a jockey he became a trainer, his horse *Psidium* won the 1961 Derby. He achieved further, unsought, fame when his name became the Cockney 'rhyming slang'

for a 'fag' (meaning cigarette). The Kinks (my favourite 1960's pop group) recorded a satirical song about cigarette smoking with the title 'Harry Rag' on their 1967 album *Something Else by the Kinks*. (For graves of famous racehorses see *A History of Suffolk Gravestones* pages 96-97.)

Robert Fiske ('Bob') Spalding won the formula one powerboat world championship in 1980 and 1985. Throughout his professional career he was nicknamed 'Mr. Nice' for his good manners, sportsmanship and modest demeanour. After retiring from racing he developed the 'Bob Spalding Marine and Outdoor Centre' in Ipswich. His headstone in Chelmondiston churchyard pays tribute to his sporting achievements.

Maurice Coreth (or Count Maurice Rudolf Coreth von und zu Coredo und Starkenberg to give him his full title) was the son of Austrian aristocrats who moved to England to escape the threat of Nazism. An accomplished horse rider, field sportsman and big game hunter in Africa, he later ran a charter boat service in the Indian Ocean. Settling in Suffolk he joined a group of former big game hunters. When they organised a lecture on the Kenyan black rhinoceros, whose numbers had declined to 300, he formed 'Rhino Rescue', organising a project to surround Lake Nakuru National Park in Kenya with a poacher proof electric fence. He went on to perform valuable conservation work in Africa and India. His gravestone in Aldeburgh churchyard displays a relief carving by his son, Mark Coreth, a wildlife sculptor. In 2009 Rhino Rescue was merged into 'Save the Rhino International' (which includes Mark Coreth among its patrons) ensuring that the valuable work initiated by Maurice Coreth continues into the twenty first century.

Benjamin Britten and Peter Pears's graves in Aldeburgh churchyard are the most visited graves in Suffolk, the only ones in the county to be signposted. Born in Lowestoft, Benjamin Britten began composing music at eleven. At 21 he collaborated with W. H. Auden on classic musical documentaries *The Coal Face* and *The Night Mail*. Three years later Benjamin met Peter Pears, a member of the B.B.C. Singers. They became lifelong companions, sharing a bond which remained an open secret (within an artistic ethos that maintained a liberal approach to such relationships) many of Benjamin's compositions were written to be sung by Peter. With the approach of the Second World War pacifist beliefs led Benjamin and Peter to move to North America. Reading *The Borough*, George Crabbe's cynical literary account of Aldeburgh, awoke Benjamin's homesickness and a desire to write *Peter Grimes*, an opera based on an episode in the poem. Returning to England, Benjamin and Peter registered as conscientious objectors, and agreed to give concerts for the 'Home Front'. For the rest of their lives they lived in Aldeburgh, gaining inspiration from the surrounding area. The debut of *Peter Grimes*, the first English opera to enter the worldwide repertoire, with Peter Pears singing the lead role, established Benjamin Britten as a leading figure in twentieth century classical music. Further successes included *Three Church Parables*, (*Curlew River*, *The Burning Fiery Furnace* and *The Prodigal Son*) portrayed in stained glass in Aldeburgh church; *Albert Herring*, a comic opera set in Suffolk; and *War Requiem*, a setting of Wilfred Owen's poetry composed for the consecration of Coventry Cathedral (see pages 24-5). Benjamin wrote *A Young Person's Guide to the Orchestra* and *Let's Make an Opera* to introduce young people to classical music. Benjamin and Peter developed the Aldeburgh Festival, for which they converted the semi-derelict Snape Maltings (see page 46) into a world renowned arts centre, turning the area into a musical rendezvous.

Imogen Holst, the only child of the composer Gustav Holst, was a leading interpreter of her father's music. A highly respected music teacher, her *ABC of Music* is a standard guide to music theory. During the Second World War she helped refugee musicians from Nazi occupied Europe and promoted musical activities to boost morale. She moved to Aldeburgh to become Benjamin Britten's musical assistant, artistic director of the Aldeburgh Festival and conductor of the Purcell Singers. Her grave stands immediately behind those of Benjamin Britten and Peter Pears at Aldeburgh: the epitaph 'the heavenly spheres make music for us, all things join in the dance' is taken from her father's *Hymn of Jesus*.

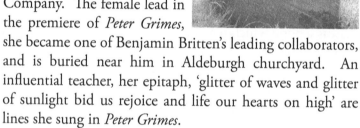

Joan Cross was the principal soprano and director of the Sadler's Wells Opera Company. The female lead in the premiere of *Peter Grimes*, she became one of Benjamin Britten's leading collaborators, and is buried near him in Aldeburgh churchyard. An influential teacher, her epitaph, 'glitter of waves and glitter of sunlight bid us rejoice and life our hearts on high' are lines she sung in *Peter Grimes*.

Martin Fallas Shaw worked with Ellen Terry's stage company (nearly marrying her daughter, Edith, before Ellen Terry disrupted the affair out of jealousy) and was conductor for the dancer Isadora Duncan. He compiled *The Oxford Book of Carols* with Ralph Vaughan Williams, and composed tunes for the hymns 'Through the night of doubt and sorrow' and 'Hills of the north rejoice'. He passed the Irish tune 'Bunessan' to the poet Eleanor Farjeon, who wrote lyrics for it with the title 'Morning has broken'; forty years later an international hit record for pop singer Cat Stevens. Martin Shaw's love of Southwold began after being sent there to cure a childhood illness. He lived there for the last years of his life, after which his ashes were interred in a cremation plot on the north side of Southwold churchyard.

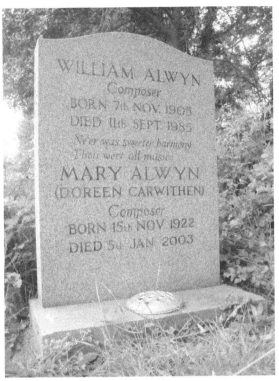

William Alwyn won a place at London's Royal Academy of Music at fifteen, financing his studies by playing in cinemas. After graduation he became a teacher at the Academy and principal flautist with the London Symphony Orchestra. While composing symphonies, he was best known for film soundtracks (his early experiences as a cinema pianist must have put him in good stead for this). He scored over a hundred films, including Carol Reed's *Odd Man Out*, (regarded as his best work), *Desert Victory*, The *Rake's Progress*, *The History of Mr. Polly*, *Mandy* and *Geordie*. Throughout his life he maintained a vigorous campaign to advance musicians' professional standing and remuneration. Doreen Mary Carwithen (who preferred her middle name) met William Alwyn while a student at the Royal Academy of Music. She, too, composed film scores, most notably for the official film of the Coronation. In 1961 they set up home in Blythburgh, where William translated French poetry and painted, while Mary composed her *Suffolk Suite*, although they did not marry until 1975; they were buried in Blythburgh churchyard. In his diary for April 15th 1956 William wrote:

'I came across these lines by William Strode (1600-1645 - my favourite period) which I would be proud to claim for my epitaph:

Ne'er was sweeter harmony;
Thou wert all music.'

While William Strode is a little known poet, the quote, from 'The latest lullaby (to Mistress Mary Prideaux)', would be a brilliant epitaph for any musician.

Maria Korchinska was born to an aristocratic Russian family: she studied at the Moscow Conservatoire, where she decided it would improve her career to specialise in the harp, since there were comparatively few harpists. She received the Conservatoire's gold medal, and joined its teaching staff. After the Russian Revolution, despite her family background, she was shown favour by Lenin and the leaders of the Bolsehvik Party, who admired classical music and were ideologically committed to developing cultural awareness among the proletariat; she played the harp at Lenin's funeral. Her husband, Nicholas Benckendorff, a diplomat's son, emigrated to England to escape the Stalinist regime; she followed him,

bringing only her daughter and two harps. Otfrid Foerster, Lenin's German doctor, organised her exit visa because he was in love with her! During the Second World War she maintained an exhausting schedule giving morale boosting concerts. The founder of the United Kingdom Harp Association, Arnold Bax dedicated his *Sonata for Harp and Viola* to her. She and her husband settled at Claydon, near expatriate relatives, and she is buried in Claydon churchyard. (See *A History of Suffolk Gravestones* page 72)

David Martin and Frederick Grinke were born in Winnipeg, Canada. They were awarded scholarships to the Royal Academy of Music in London, where they met Florence Hooton, a cello student from Scarborough in Yorkshire: all three became distinguished teachers at the Academy, performing and recording together in various combinations or as part of larger ensembles. Florence and David married in 1938; Arnold Bax dedicated his *Legend Sonata* to Florence. Frederick became concertmaster of the Boyd Neel Orchestra, during the Second World War he played for Churchill, Stalin and Truman at the Potsdam Conference. They are

buried by the exceptionally beautiful small parish church of Thornham Parva.

Clifford Grey was born Percival Davis in Birmingham: he took Clifford Grey as a stage name, using this for the rest of his life, although never legally changing it. He was a prolific author of librettos and scores for stage and cinema, including two of the most successful musicals of the 1920's, *Mr. Cinders* (which included the song 'Spread a little happiness', revived as a U.K chart hit by the pop singer *Sting* in 1982) and *Sally*. He wrote lyrics for over 3,000 songs, the most famous of which was undoubtedly 'If you were the only girl in the world (and I was the only boy)'. Another composition was 'Got a date with an angel'. In 1941 he was performing for the Entertainments National Service Association (E.N.S.A.) in Ipswich when the town was bombed. The shock of this may have caused medical complications leading to his demise two days later; he was buried in Ipswich Old Cemetery in Belvedere Road (plot H). After his death it was discovered that he had invented a second, fictitious persona for himself as 'Tippi Grey' when he joined with three athletic friends to form the U.S. bobsleigh team, winning gold medals in the 1928 and 1932 winter Olympics. His grave was recently renovated by relatives and admirers to give him some of the appreciation which was thought to be his due.

John Robert Parker Ravenscroft, better known as John Peel, was born in Burton on Merseyside. Moving to the U.S.A. he worked as a presenter on local radio stations from 1960, with the advent of 'Beatlemania' his Liverpool origins greatly increased his popularity. Returning to England he became a disc jockey for Radio London, one of the 'pirate radio' stations that circumvented broadcasting rules by operating from ships outside British territorial waters. Here he developed his trademark dry humour and deadpan style of vocal delivery. When it was suggested that he find a more memorable and catchy surname than Ravenscroft, a secretary casually suggested 'Peel'. After the government ended pirate radio 'John Peel' was offered a late night 'slot' on the new Radio One (he remains its longest serving presenter). He gave many pop musicians and groups their first exposure,

including Pink Floyd and Marc Bolan (he appeared on Marc Bolan's *Unicorn* album.) In 1974 he married Sheila Gilhooly: they moved to Great Finborough, where they called their house *Peel Acres*: he broadcast many radio programmes from his home studio there. He later presented *Home Truths*, a radio programme exploring humorous aspects of domestic life. Dying unexpectedly while on holiday in Peru, his funeral in the Cathedral in Bury St. Edmunds was packed with figures from the pop music and entertainment world. Stowmarket Corn Exchange has been converted into the *John Peel Centre for Creative Arts* in tribute to his memory. He is buried in Great Finborough churchyard. The 'Liver Bird', on his gravestone derives from his lifelong support of Liverpool Football Club, (his children had middle names derived from the club). The line 'teenage dreams so hard to beat' was taken from 'Teenage kicks', his favourite record (released by the pop group *The Undertones* in 1977) which he had requested to be inscribed on his memorial.

Derek Wyn Taylor was born in Liverpool. In 1963, as newspaper reporter, he was sent to cover a concert by the Beatles. Instructed to dismiss them as a passing fad, instead they so impressed him that he used his journalistic credentials to cultivate their friendship. He became personal assistant and press agent to Brian Epstein, the Beatles' manager, ghost-writing Brian Epstein's 'autobiography' *A Cellarful of Noise*. He wrote the sleeve notes for the *Beatles for Sale* and *Yellow Submarine* albums and sent Harry

Nilsson's early records to the Beatles, initiating their friendship and collaborations. Moving to California, Derek became the publicity agent for the Beach Boys, the Byrds and Buffalo Springfield, while helping to organise the 1967 Monterey Pop Festival. He is mentioned in the fourth verse of John Lennon's 'Give peace a chance'; he inadvertently inspired George Harrison's song 'Blue Jay Way' (from the *Magical Mystery Tour* album): he got lost going to Blue Jay Way in Los Angeles to meet George, who composed the song waiting for him to arrive. In the 1970's Derek moved to Brundon Mill near Sudbury, while avoiding publicity, he assisted in writing George Harrison's autobiography *I, Me, Mine*, and co-operated with the massively popular *Beatles Anthology* project. When he was buried in the public cemetery in Newton Road, Sudbury, many figures from the music industry attended his funeral.

When researching this book I discovered a gravestone with a previously unrecognised link to the Beatles' album, *Sergeant Pepper's Lonely Hearts Club Band*, frequently nominated as the best 'LP' ever made. John Henderson's headstone stands southwest of the chapel in Ipswich Old Cemetery (plot C). (The burial is recorded in the cemetery registers.) While the inscription is badly worn, the name 'John Henderson' can be deciphered. He was a gymnast and horse-rider for Pablo Fanque (Britain's first black circus proprietor) before starting his own circus. On 20 April 1867 the *Ipswich Journal* announced the arrival of 'Henderson's Royal Circus'. John Henderson died suddenly of pleurisy 10 May, aged only 45. His obituary on 18 May reported 'as a circus manager he conducted his performances in a very respectable manner, and as an equestrian and gymnast he has been a great public favourite', whose funeral attracted 'thousands' (presumably from the fairground community) to Ipswich.

In 1967 John Lennon bought a circus poster, advertising an appearance of Pablo Fanque's Fair in Rochdale, when 'Mr. J. Henderson, the celebrated somerset (somersault) thrower, wire dancer, vaulter, rider' headed the bill. While John Lennon knew nothing about the people on the poster, he rewrote the billing as a song, 'Being for the benefit of Mr. Kite' for the Beatles' *Sergeant Pepper's Lonely Hearts' Club Band* LP. John Lennon changed 'John Henderson' to 'The Hendersons' to improve scansion, mentioning them four times. The Beatles guaranteed John Henderson a place in musical history. It is tempting to wonder if the horse on John Henderson's gravestone is 'Henry the Horse' who is mentioned in the song.

DISASTERS

There are three memorials to disasters in Ipswich Old Cemetery in Belvedere Road. The Ipswich schooner *Petrel* left Middlesbrough on 27 October 1884, bound for Ipswich with a cargo of pig iron. Next day she floundered in a storm off Flamborough Head. The storm was so severe that the local lifeboat could not reach the Petrel, which sunk with the loss of all four crew members: the captain, Arthur Bowman (also lessee of the bathing place in Fore Street, Ipswich), his son, Ernest (the mate) and two local seamen, Walter Halls and William Norman: the first three left widows and children. A memorial to the Petrel and her crew stands in plot F.

On 25 September 1900 John Barnard was driving a railway engine from Ipswich Station, accompanied by his fireman, William MacDonald. Just before they reached Westerfield Station the engine's boiler burst with a massive explosion, flying 120 feet through the air before hitting the ground and bouncing into a porter's hut which shattered with the impact. Two of the train's wheels were buried in the ground. John was found 150 feet away, while William was discovered in a wagon at the end of the train: both were probably killed instantaneously. Two people nearby were wounded by flying debris. At an enquiry it was found that the boiler had been leaking badly and the engine was not safe to drive. John and William's funeral was attended by 200 railway employees. Their graves stand on the west side of the footpath from the Belvedere Road entrance to the cemetery chapels (plot I).

Thomas Balaam was a shedman and shunter at the Great Eastern Railway depot in Croft Street in Ipswich. The *Ipswich Journal* of 24 June 1919 says his decapitated body was found on a railway track outside the depot. It appeared that he had been hit by a railway train, and had somehow fallen underneath it in such a way that his head was cut off. An experienced railway employee of 63, it seems that he was the victim of a bizarre freak accident. A coroner's court declared a verdict of accidental death, for which nobody was to blame. A small headstone in his memory stands in plot X.

Harry Read, a 26 year old fireman for the Great Eastern Railway, lived at 5 Stevens Street, near Lowestoft Railway Station, with his wife and two year old son. On Christmas Eve in 1891 he was part of the crew of a train travelling from Lowestoft to Beccles. At Barnby, midway between these towns, the railway line merged into a single track, with a loop where trains could pass. Night had fallen, a thick, low-lying fog had formed. Shortly after 6.35pm the signalman saw a goods train pushing a tender coming eastward from Beccles. As this began moving into the loop the Lowestoft-Beccles passenger train appeared, hurtling westward through the fog. In panic the signalman pulled the stop signals on the westbound track. Although the express crew applied the brakes they collided into the goods train: there was an immense impact and both trains rolled over off the line. The shock was terrifying for the passengers, whose confusion and panic was intensified by the darkness and fog; thirty six of them required hospital treatment for injuries. Harry Read and two other members of the train crews were killed. Harry Read was buried in Lowestoft Cemetery in Normanston Road, where his fellow railway workers paid for this memorial (plot 6, grave 131).

The headstone next to Harry Read's memorial (plot 7, grave 140) commemorates Arthur Press, a 36 year old railway guard, who lived with his wife and daughter at 24 Bevan Street West, near Lowestoft Station. On 7 January 1894 he was killed while on duty at Norwich Thorpe Station. I have not found many details of his death in newspaper reports, but the *Lowestoft Journal* of 13 January 1894 suggests that it was felt by his railway colleagues, since six carriages were required to bring people to the funeral.

Sidney Keeble was the fireman of the Cromer Express. On Saturday 12 July 1913 the train was returning to King's Cross: near Colchester it was directed onto a railway line behind a light engine. As the first driver frantically moved his locomotive into top speed the Express crew slammed their brakes on, but the trains were too close and collided. In the last few seconds the driver of the light engine jumped from his train, but the Express crew stayed at their posts. Sidney Keeble was killed, as was George Burdett the guard, while William Barnard, the driver, expired on the way to the hospital (by a sad stroke of fate he was the son of John Barnard who died in the Westerfield railway explosion) (*See page 77*). Some passengers on the Cromer Express were injured, but none died: by staying at their posts the crew may have averted more casualties. Sidney Keeble lived in Ipswich (where he was a member of the ambulance brigade), but as he came from Bramford he was buried in the churchyard of his home parish.

On 1st June 1914 five Sea Scouts, aged between 14 and 19, went on a weekend camp at Somerleyton, with Thomas Lory, a solicitor (the Sea Scouts' district secretary) and James Lewington, a railway worker and former royal navy seaman. They were returning to Oulton Broad on a sailing boat, which dipped and sank: one scout, Stanley Wood, swum to shore and ran for help. Several boats came to the scene, but the vessel had submerged and the other six occupants drowned. Blinds in the area were drawn and flags flown at half-mast in mourning. Stanley Wood was killed at the Battle of the Somme two years later. In 1918 the Bishop of Norwich unveiled this memorial to the scouts in the cemetery in St. Peter's Road in Carlton Colville.

Violet Jessop survived sinking of both the *Titanic* and the *Britannic*. Born to Irish parents who emigrated to Argentina, at sixteen she became an ocean liner stewardess. At 24 she served on the *Titanic*. She was in bed in her cabin when the ship gave a dull shudder and stopped moving. As a sense of alarm circulated she dressed and came to the deck, not comprehending how anything could go wrong with such a wonderful ship. A male crew member ushered her onto a lifeboat carrying immigrant passengers, one of whom gave her a baby to hold. As the lifeboat was lowered to the sea and pulled away she sat transfixed by the Titanic's lights until they went out and the liner vanished below the water in the darkening night. Next morning her lifeboat was rescued by the *Carpathia*. As she got on board somebody snatched the baby;

she never saw the child or its family again. In 1916 she worked on the *Britannic*, a liner converted into a hospital ship, which was sunk by a mine while crossing the Aegean Sea. (Fortunately the *Britannic* was going to collect injured soldiers, so there were no sick or wounded on board.) Putting on a lifejacket Violet jumped into the sea: striking the side of the ship she was nearly pulled under before being dragged to safety. Her autobiography, *Titanic Survivor*, was published in 1997. After retirement she lived in Great Ashfield; she is buried in the cemetery in Shimpling Road in Hartest.

On 7 December 1899 the Aldeburgh lifeboat, called The *Aldeburgh*, was launched to rescue a vessel which had run aground on the Shipwash Sands. Eighteen men, captained by Charles Ward, steered into a strong easterly gale and heavy surf. The *Aldeburgh* overturned on a sandbar, twelve of the crew were thrown into the sea, but six were trapped under the boat. Charles Ward was washed ashore, although badly shaken he repeatedly returned into the heavy surf to help his comrades to land, then took the lead in trying to upturn the lifeboat and chop a hole into the hull to release those trapped underneath. He received the R.N.L.I. silver medal for his heroism. The six men trapped under the boat were drowned, a seventh later died from injuries. They were buried before this memorial, the largest in Aldeburgh churchyard, a testimony to the heroism of all lifeboatmen who regularly risk death or injury, with no financial reward, to save the lives of others.

This final chapter illustrates memorials to some other people who contributed to history, or whose stories throw light on the past.

Martha Crane's gravestone stands against the east perimeter wall of the Great Churchyard in Bury St. Edmunds. The epitaph says 'she had the honour to be midwife to the late Queen Caroline and brought three of the royal family into the world'. The queen referred to is Caroline of Ansbach, who was born in Germany, where she married the future George II in 1705. Caroline moved to England in 1714, when her father-in-law became George I of England, and her husband the Prince Of Wales. The three members of the royal family mentioned are therefore probably Caroline and George II's youngest children, William, the Duke Of Cumberland; Mary, who married the Landgrave Of Hesse Kassel (an unhappy marriage that ended in divorce); and Louise, who became Queen of Denmark and Norway.

A small gravestone on the north side of Akenham church is a reminder of the Akenham Burial Case of 1878. Joseph, the son of Edward and Sarah Ramsey, died aged two. As Baptists the Ramseys believed in adult baptism, so Joseph had not been baptised. Under canon law an unbaptised person could not be buried with Church of England rites, but George Drury, the rector of Akenham, had to accompany the coffin to the grave and record the burial in the parish register. It is agreed that an unusually long funeral ceremony was held outside the churchyard, leading to a bad tempered altercation between George Drury and some of those present. *The East Anglian Daily Times* published a hostile article, based on received information rather than eyewitness accounts, describing how a clergyman disrupted a child's funeral with demands for a quick burial. George Drury sued the editor of the *East Anglian Daily Times* for libel, saying the event was misreported. He was duty bound to attend the funeral, which continued for an inordinately long time. When he reasonably asked if the coffin could be committed to the grave, so he could leave, he was met with abuse and hostility. While the court awarded George Drury £2 damages, a fund set up to pay the newspaper's legal costs received over £1,000, some of which was used to pay for Joseph Ramsey's gravestone. Although George Drury has often been portrayed as the villain of the drama, he was a proponent of the 'Tractarian' or 'Anglo-Catholic' movement, which sought to revive ceremony and ritual in the Church of England, a controversial policy at the time. It has been suggested that the funeral was staged by some of his opponents to antagonise, and thus discredit him. The publicity surrounding the Akenham Burial Case helped bring about the 'Burial Laws Amendment Act' of 1880, allowing all religious denominations to hold funerals in parish churchyards.

Two important people, Thomas Clarkson and George Biddell Airy, are buried side by side in Playford churchyard. Thomas Clarkson was arguably the leading British anti-slavery activist. Planning to become a clergyman, after entering a contest to write a Latin essay on slavery he decided to dedicate his life to ending slavery in the British Empire. He pioneered many of the activities used by modern pressure groups: collecting case studies of the mistreatment of slaves; distributing graphics and images showing the horrors of slavery; organising anti-slavery petitions to the government; and calling for what would now be called 'trade boycotts' when people refused to buy items produced by slave labour. After numerous demoralising set-backs he saw the abolition of the slave trade within the British Empire in 1807, followed by the abolition of slavery itself in 1833. Frederick Hervey of Ickworth, the first Marquess of Bristol, a great admirer, gave him Playford Hall as a residence, where he died in 1846. Thomas's wife, Catherine, was regarded as a fascinating, intelligent and knowledgeable conversationalist: she encouraged the literary careers of William Wordsworth and Samuel Taylor Coleridge. Harriet Beecher Stowe, author of the seminal anti-slavery novel, *Uncle Tom's Cabin*, made a pilgrimage to Playford to meet Catherine and visit

Thomas Clarkson's grave. Catherine was buried alongside Thomas (and their son, also called Thomas, who predeceased them). Thomas Clarkson was attracted to Quakerism (Quakers were prominent in the anti-slavery movement) he shared that belief's system's disapproval of churchyard memorials. Railings were later placed around his burial plot; an obelisk in his memory has been erected in Playford churchyard.

As a youth George Biddell Airy met Thomas Clarkson while staying with relations at Playford. Thomas Clarkson recognised his intelligence and helped secure his entry to Cambridge University, where he became professor of astronomy at 26. Appointed Astronomer Royal at 34, he re-equipped the Royal Observatory at Greenwich with instruments he designed himself, including the 'Transit Circle', the telescope which defines the Greenwich Meridian and Greenwich Mean Time. Investigating his poor eyesight, he was the first person to identify *astigmatism* and make glasses to correct it. He formulated the 'Airy function', a mathematical equation used in quantum mechanics and advanced physics. President of the Royal Society and the Royal Astronomical Society, he was knighted in 1872. He had a country house at Playford and was buried beside his wife, Richarda, (described as a great beauty in her youth) and three of their children. His other memorials include craters on Mars, *Airy* and *Airy* O, which define the prime meridian on that planet.

Thomas Clarkson's younger brother, John Clarkson, a naval officer, was drawn into the anti-slavery movement. During the American War of Independence slaves were offered freedom if they helped the British army. The *Sierra Leone Company* was formed to return these freed slaves to Africa, to start a colony and trading base. In 1791 John was chosen to command a fleet taking 1,196 African Americans to establish *Freetown* in Sierra Leone: this was, for better or for worse, the first British colonial venture in Africa. John treated African Americans as equal to Whites and encouraged them to run Freetown themselves. This brought him into conflict with the directors of the Sierra Leone Company who wanted to run Freetown as a profit making institution (even if this meant denying the Blacks political and economic independence). His stance led to his dismissal, while he never returned to Sierra Leone, many colonists held him in high esteem. He became manager of Alexander's Bank in Woodbridge, where he was buried west of St. Mary's church.

James Edward Smith was the son of a wealthy Unitarian wool merchant in Norwich. When he was 24 Carl Linnaeus's botanical collections, the largest assembled to that date, were offered for sale, and he bought them with a £900 loan from his father. Linnaeus, a Swedish academic, is regarded as the founder of scientific plant taxonomy; possession of his collections made James Europe's most respected and sought after botanist. He wrote profusely (including a 36 volume *English Botany*), tutored members of the royal family (which helped him to receive a

knighthood) and founded the Linnaean Society of London. Marrying Pleasance Reeve, the daughter of a Lowestoft lawyer and merchant, he was buried in her family vault in St. Margaret's churchyard in Lowestoft. After James's death Pleasance (the great-aunt of Alice Pleasance Liddell, for whom Lewis Carroll wrote *Alice in Wonderland*) edited his writings, while maintaining an active scientific and literary correspondence. Living to be 103, she remains a folk heroine in Lowestoft.

John Stevens Henslow was professor of botany at Cambridge, where he pioneered the use of practical experiments and field trips, devised 'plant sampling' and set up the Botanical Gardens (my family's favourite garden of all those we have visited)! Appointed rector of Hitcham in 1837, at a time when many university academics simply took clerical posts for the income these provided, he moved to the village and actively involved himself in parish life. He set up allotments for the villagers, organised some of the earliest village fetes, ran botanical activities for children, and introduced farmers to new scientific agricultural methods. At Felixstowe he discovered *coprolite*, a mineral deposit with high phosphate content, leading to the development of the Suffolk fertiliser industry, with factories in Ipswich, Stowmarket and Bramford. He excavated Eastlow Hill, a Roman burial mound at Rougham, publishing a detailed record of his discoveries, Suffolk's first scientific excavation, leading him to be hailed as the founding father of Suffolk archaeology.

As Charles Darwin's tutor at Cambridge John Stevens Henslow recommended Darwin as the naturalist to accompany the scientific survey of the South American coast in the barque H.M.S. Beagle, where Darwin formulated the theory of evolution. Henslow's last public duty was to chair the 'Oxford Evolution Debate' of 1860, when Thomas Huxley's defence of Darwin against the Bishop of Oxford's ridicule led to the scientific community's acceptance of evolution. When Charles Darwin wished to acquire plant specimens for study he often contacted Henslow for items the children of Hitcham had collected and identified. John Stevens Henslow was buried near the west (tower) door of Hitcham church. The inscription on his memorial is difficult to decipher, as it is covered by moss. As a keen bryologist John Stevens Henslow might have approved of this.

John Ellor Taylor, the son of a Lancashire millworker, became a journalist, writing popular books about science. In 1872 he was invited to become curator of the Ipswich Museum, which was deteriorating and attracting few visitors; he revived it, moving it to its present premises in the High Street. He gave popular lectures (declining payment if they were for working class audiences) and helped start the *East Anglian Daily Times*. Running into financial difficulties (possibly exacerbated by alcoholism) he was declared bankrupt and forced to resign his curatorship two years before his death, when he was buried in Ipswich Old Cemetery (plot C).

Duleep Singh was the son of Ranjit Singh 'the Lion of the Punjab'. When he was eleven the Anglo-Sikh wars led to the British conquest of the Punjab, when he had to resign his sovereignty with the royal treasury and estates. The fairness (and legality) of this, and his subsequent treatment was questionable. While receiving a large allowance and an excellent education, he was removed from the Punjab, his freedom was restricted, and he was inculcated with European values, only being allowed to meet Europeans or westernised Indians, causing him to accept Christianity. At sixteen he went to Britain,

where his looks and manners captivated Queen Victoria. He only returned to India to bring his mother to England, and for her funeral. During his second trip he visited Egypt, where he married Bamba Muller, a sixteen year old mission school teacher, the daughter of a German father and an Abyssinian mother. Queen Victoria treated Bamba as an equal (they were both queens)! Duleep and Bamba acquired the Elveden Estate, where they were exemplary landlords. Duleep had Elveden Hall rebuilt with an authentically Indian interior, turning the estate into one of Britain's best game preserves. He was an expert shot and the Prince of Wales visited his sporting parties. Like the Prince of Wales, Duleep was a serial philanderer, notorious for expenditure on high class London courtesans. Becoming resentful of British control Duleep decided to return to the Punjab where he and Bamba would assume their rightful role as the leaders of the Sikhs, but they were stopped at Aden. Embittered by this, Duleep went into voluntary exile in Paris. Bamba returned to Elveden where she died eighteen months later. On his death in 1893 Duleep was buried at Elveden. His grave (foreground) stands alongside that of Bamba (centre) and their youngest son, Albert Edward, who died aged ten (background). In 1993 a plaque honouring his Sikh heritage was placed on Elveden church, in 1999 his statue was unveiled in Thetford. The Sikh community, which has provided many soldiers for the British army, and made an important contribution to British life, regard his grave as a centre of pilgrimage.

John Spencer Login was born in Stromness in the Orkney Islands. He was admitted to Edinburgh University to study medicine when aged 15. After taking his MD degree at 21 he was offered a post with the East India Company. He received rapid promotion within the organisation, becoming resident surgeon at Lucknow, then physician and postmaster to the court at Oudh. After serving in the Second Sikh War he was appointed guardian to the young Duleep Singh, and placed in charge of the treasury of the Sikh Empire. Regarded as highly conscientious and trustworthy (in an organisation whose members were frequently accused of lining their pockets) while both posts presented incredible opportunities for self-enrichment, he took nothing more than his official salary for his duties, which included

transferring the *Koh-I-Noor*, the world's largest diamond, from the Sikh Treasury to British officials, who conveyed it to Queen Victoria, to form part of the crown jewels. He treated the young Duleep liberally, and the two became very close, although the maharajah's 'westernisation' is now a controversial subject. After taking Duleep to meet Queen Victoria, who knighted John in appreciation of his treatment of the maharajah, John bought a house at Felixstowe, but returned to India to investigate the state of the country after the Indian Mutiny and improve the railway network. He died suddenly and unexpectedly in his Felixstowe home in 1863. Hearing of this Duleep Singh exclaimed 'Oh I have lost my father! For he was indeed that, and more to me'. Duleep paid for his memorial in St. Peter and St. Paul's churchyard in Felixstowe.

Horace Reynolds, familiarly known as 'Poll' was an eccentric Woodbridge character. With the advent of the motor car Cross Corner at Woodbridge became a notorious congestion spot. Horace, a barge hand, took it on himself to direct traffic there with a flag, wearing a self-made uniform (and a coat given by the fifth Baron Rendlesham, of Rendlesham Hall). His services were voluntary, and he lived off tips from passers-by. On his death in 1910 the *Woodbridge Reporter* wrote 'it is almost safe to say that never before has anyone occupying so humble a position in the town been shewn such spontaneous and genuine sympathy'. His gravestone, in Woodbridge Old Cemetery, in Warren Hill Road, was paid for by public collection.

The Quilter family monument stands in Bawdsey churchyard. Originating from Trimley, the Quilters became wealthy London stockbrokers and accountants. In 1883 Sir William Cuthbert Quilter, the first baronet, a Liberal M.P., bought the Bawdsey estate because of family connections with the area. He had Bawdsey Manor built, and improved the village, instituting a ferry to Felixstowe, and establishing a stud for Suffolk Punch horses. Four of these (Prince, Prosperine, Valliant and Violet) drew his body to the grave. Several of his descendants are buried here, including Roger and John Raymond Cuthbert Quilter. Roger Quilter, a composer, wrote music for young people, including the *Children's Overture* and a children's opera, *Where the Rainbow Ends* (once a popular theatrical production). A founder of the Musician's Benevolent Fund, Roger helped

Jewish musicians escape Nazi occupied Europe. John Raymond Cuthbert (normally known as Raymond) the third baronet, founded the GQ Parachute Company, Britain's leading parachute manufacturer during the Second World War, designing many of its products himself. The Quilter family bought Lavenham Guildhall to preserve it, presenting it to

the National Trust. During the Second World War Bawdsey Manor was the national centre for radar research and development: individually and collectively the Quilters have been most beneficial to Suffolk. (See *A History of Suffolk Gravestones* page 97.)

Glencairn Stuart Ogilvie (better known as Stuart Ogilvie) was the son of Alexander Ogilvie, a Scotsman who made a large fortune as a railway entrepreneur. The Ogilvies bought Sizewell Hall, near the Suffolk coast, and acquired land in the surrounding countryside. Stuart wrote plays, most notably a highly successful dramatisation of Charles Kingsley's novel *Hypatia*. In 1908 Stuart inherited the Ogilvie family estates, which included the Suffolk coastal hamlet of Thorpe. Stuart conceived the idea of

turning Thorpe into a fantasy holiday village, and personally supervised the transformation, renaming it *Thorpeness*. The idyllic, unconventional community of Thorpeness, full of unusual, individual buildings centred on *The Meare* (a large boating lake, landscaped by Stuart) is a monument to his vision. Stuart was buried in Aldringham churchyard, where the Ogilvie family plot forms one of the most impressive groups of memorials in any Suffolk churchyard.

Mary Cecil was born Mary Rothes Margaret Tyssen-Amherst, the daughter of William, Baron Amherst of Hackney. Her family were keen Egyptologists: Mary directed excavations in Egypt, discovering *The Cecil Tombs* an important burial sequence. (Since renamed the *Tombs of the Nobles* or *Qubbet el Hawa*.) After she published *Bird Notes from the Nile* the black crowned crane was named the *balearica pavonia ceciliae* in her honour. She was awarded the O.B.E. for her work to maintain and improve sanitation and health in Britain during the First World War. As her father had no sons he made provisions that she inherited his peerage in her own right. She married William Cecil, a son of the Marquess of Exeter, they lived in Stowlangtoft Hall and are buried in Stowlangtoft churchyard.

Jane Walker was among the first Englishwomen to qualify as a doctor (after Elizabeth Garrett Anderson, see page 46) having to take a degree in Brussels. At Nayland she opened the East Anglian Sanatorium, the first English hospital to apply 'open air treatment' for Tuberculosis sufferers. The first president of the Medical Women's Foundation, George VI appointed her a Companion of Honour (an award restricted to 65 outstanding public servants). She was buried in Wissington churchyard. After the eradication of tuberculosis in the United Kingdom the East Anglian Sanatorium, just within view of Wissington church, was converted into private houses, with the name Jane Walker Park.

Edith Pretty, the daughter of Robert Dempster, a Manchester industrialist, was a nurse with the Royal Army Medical Corps during the First World War, and an active charity worker. At 18 she met Frank Pretty, a member of the Ipswich family of clothing manufacturers, but they did not marry until she was 43, when they moved to Tranmer House in Sutton. He died eight years later, in 1934. In 1938 Edith enlisted Basil Brown, a Suffolk archaeologist, to investigate mounds at Sutton Hoo, near her house. The following story, culminating in the discovery of an astonishing Anglo-Saxon ship burial, is one of the great romances of British archaeology. Edith Pretty gave the finds from Sutton Hoo to the British Museum, without asking for payment, even declining Winston Churchill's offer of the award of a Commander of the British Empire (C.B.E.) in gratitude for her generosity. The Ipswich based Eastern Angles Theatre Company staged *The Sutton Hoo Mob*, an excellent dramatisation of the events surrounding the excavation. In this Edith Pretty felt that since the treasure had been deposited by a king of East Anglia it should be returned to a greater power, in this case the nation of England. Edith Pretty was buried with her husband in Sutton churchyard. Tranmer House and the site of the Sutton Hoo excavations are now owned by the National Trust so that the public can appreciate the environment in which she lived and in which the archaeological discoveries were made.

Robert Grenville (better known as 'John') and Thomas Gayer Anderson were twin brothers. John became a doctor with the Royal Army Medical Corps in Egypt. Thomas served in the Boer War and First World War, becoming a Colonel; during the Second World War he co-ordinated the Home Guard. Even when separated, twins' lives often follow similar paths. John acquired the seventeenth century 'Beit-al-Kritliyya' (House of the Cretan

Woman), in Cairo, turning it into a museum. Thomas restored Little Hall at Lavenham, a medieval merchant's house, laying out a beautiful garden. King Farouk of Egypt awarded John the rank of 'Lewa' (Major-General) and title of Pasha for services to Egyptian art and culture. Retiring to Lavenham, John donated much of his collection of ancient Egyptian antiquities to the Fitzwilliam Museum in Cambridge, reserving a bronze statue, *the Gayer Anderson Cat*, for the British Museum, where it is a popular item in the Egyptian galleries. He was buried to the east of the chapel in the public cemetery in Bridge Street Road, in Lavenham, under a memorial displaying an Arabic inscription written by King Farouk. John wrote the epitaph:

> Here lieth that which scattereth and yet remaineth, the immortal body of a man.
> It is to the whole, the true, the beautiful pertaineth, which is 'God'.

Thomas was buried in the same grave fourteen years later. Little Hall is now the headquarters of the Suffolk Preservation Society, open to the public during the summer. (See *A History of Suffolk Gravestones*, pages 95-6.)

Alexander Sutherland Neill set up a school, called *Summerhill* after the house where it was situated, which he moved to Leiston in 1927. Summerhill is famous because pupils only have to go to lessons if they want to, and is run democratically, by meetings of pupils and teachers. Neill said his educational aim was to produce happy, balanced, fulfilled personalities, which were created by a sense of freedom. He thought rules should be laid down by common consent, rather than unquestioning acceptance of authority. A fluent and articulate writer, he expounded his ideas in books which became international best-sellers. (Knowing he would never receive universal approval, one of his books about Summerhill was entitled *That Awful School*.) Enid Blyton's *Naughtiest Girl* series of books were set in *Whyteleafe*, a progressive school openly modelled on Summerhill. C. S. Lewis satirised Summerhill in *The Silver Chair*, part of his *Chronicles of Narnia*, sections of which are set in *Experiment House*, a ludicrously mismanaged progressive school that is overthrown by a pupil rebellion. A. S. Neills's ashes were interred in the public cemetery in Waterloo Avenue in Leiston. He remains one of the twentieth century's most widely discussed educational theorists, while Summerhill is arguably the world's most famous and influential 'progressive school'.

Percy Edwards was born in Ipswich and lived in Suffolk for all of his life. As a child he was fascinated by the birds on the heaths near his home, and imitated their calls and songs to attract them. 'Bird impersonators' often appeared at variety theatres: realising that he could give better impersonations (and more accurate ornithological information) Percy began performing publicly. Capable of accurately impersonating 600 birds (and many animals) he made his radio debut at 22 and went on to make literally hundreds of radio and television appearances, becoming a nationally known entertainer. He was awarded the M.B.E. for services to entertainment and ornithology. His son ran the post office at Polstead, and he is buried on the edge of Polstead churchyard, overlooking meadows which are excellent for bird watching. (I found a blackbird's nest on a ledge in the south porch of Polstead church: it seems peculiarly appropriate that birds should shelter in the church by Percy Edwards's grave.)

Cyril Francis Bowers, better known as Monty, is buried in Little Cornard churchyard. Enquiring about him locally, I found that he started as a ploughman using horses, adapted to tractors, and worked at Grey's Hall Farm at Little Cornard into his seventies. The *East Anglian Daily Times* of 27 May 1986 contains a supplement on the Suffolk Show at Ipswich, which reports that he was to be awarded the Suffolk Agricultural Association's Long Service Award from the guest of honour, Diana Spencer. I felt he deserved inclusion in this book, as a representative of those who did not achieve fame or wealth, but whose everyday endeavours have shaped Suffolk's identity.

Goodwyn Barmby was born in Yoxford in 1820. (Baptised John Goodwin Barmby, he abandoned his forename and adapted his middle name.) In his youth he was friendly with James Bird (see page 7). Goodwyn's coming of age co-incided with an outburst of radical activity across Britain. He became an active member of the Chartist movement, which advocated full adult male suffrage; at 16 he addressed farm workers

about political emancipation. Visiting Paris in 1840 he joined discussion groups, inventing a new name for the revolutionary ideals of the time *Communism*! He wrote about Communism for English radical journals, the first time the word appeared in print. At 21 he married Catherine Isabella Watkins: she believed women should vote, an idea that even the Chartists thought too extreme to contemplate. Goodwyn and Catherine formed the *Central Communist Propaganda Society*, the first organisation to be called Communist and to campaign for female suffrage. Proclaiming 1841 the Year One, they published journals and pamphlets expounding their ideals, while attempting to set up Communist communities and a Christian Communist church. In 1848 there was a European upsurge of revolutionary upheaval. When this collapsed Goodwyn, like many radicals of the time, abandoned his early ideals, forgetting Communism to become a Unitarian minister in Devon. (The year he abandoned Communism was marked by Karl Marx's publication of *The Communist Manifesto*. It is not known if Goodwyn read Karl Marx's works.) Catherine's death in 1853 caused him to move to Wakefield, where he continued serving as a Unitarian minister, while writing pastoral and religious poetry, and supporting the Liberal Party, the Co-Operative Movement, and female suffrage. He retired to Yoxford at 59. At his death, two years later, his Unitarian beliefs precluded a Church of England funeral, so he was buried in the public cemetery in Fore Street in Framlingham. Although his headstone calls him 'preacher and poet', no editor or critic has championed, promoted or republished his verse or journalism, which was at least competent by the standards of the time (see one example on page 7). His gravestone, beside a brook in the 'Lower Cemetery', east of the Tetley family plot (see page 50), is little known. When I first came to Framlingham to look for Goodwyn Barmby's grave the cemetery caretaker had not heard of him, and had to search the cemetery register to find his memorial. It is an irony of history that while Karl Marx's grave in Highgate Cemetery is world famous, the grave of the man who invented the word Communism stands unknown in the public cemetery at Framlingham.

INDEX OF PEOPLE
MENTIONED IN THE BOOK

INDEX OF PLACES
MENTIONED IN THE BOOK

REFERENCES ARE TO PARISH CHURCHES
UNLESS OTHERWISE SPECIFIED

Lightning Source UK Ltd.
Milton Keynes UK
UKHW031008281022
411251UK00009B/607